THE FAMILY LIBRARY OF
DOGS

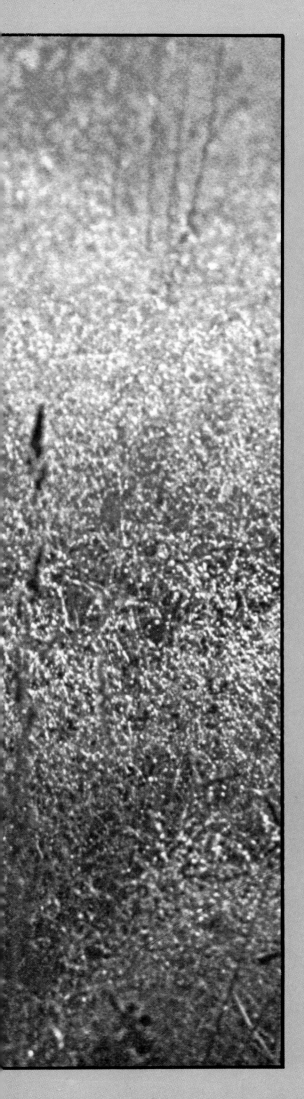

THE FAMILY LIBRARY OF
DOGS

Wendy Boorer

octopus

First published in 1981
by Octopus Books Limited
59 Grosvenor Street
London W1

©1980 Octopus Books Limited

ISBN 0 7064 1460 8

Produced for Octopus by
Theorem Publishing Limited
71-73 Great Portland Street
London W1N 5DH

Printed in Hong Kong

Introduction

Dogs have been our companions and servants for an exceptionally long time. The partnership probably began when wild dogs prowled round the camps of nomadic huntsmen 10,000 years ago. Soon the dogs joined in the hunt, and later helped tend flocks and possessions. These are both jobs that dogs continue to carry out to this day – they guard our houses, they help the police and the army, they guide the blind and, above all, they are devoted companions to millions of people.

   This guide describes many of the breeds available – sporting dogs, working dogs, giants and miniatures. It also gives expert advice on how to choose your own puppy, how to care for it and train it, and perhaps even enter it for a dog show. Your dog may not be a champion, but it will undoubtedly be a most faithful friend!

Contents

Chapter one
Man and his Dog

The beginning of the partnership between man and dog took place a very long time ago. The dog's wolf-like ancestors first prowled around human settlements scavenging for leftovers. But they soon took to helping in the hunt and our unique friendship with the dog had begun.

Dogs have been our friends for so long that now we can only guess how the partnership formed in the first place. The dog was the first domesticated animal. Wild animals fear people instinctively. Given the chance they will hide or run away and, if prevented from doing either, their fear may lead them to a desperate attack. In domesticated animals this fear has largely been lost. They are not afraid of living close to man and do not regard him as an enemy unless his behaviour towards them has been cruel and hurtful. Their fear has not entirely gone – a nervous dog will bite if it becomes very frightened – but on the whole the relationship between man and his domesticated animals is a peaceful and friendly one.

Domestication must have taken a very long time, a continuing process over many generations, and it took place so long ago that we cannot be sure exactly how it happened. Some time between 15,000 and 10,000 years ago Palaeolithic man took the first steps which were to lead to a successful partnership between man and dog. Palaeolithic man was a nomadic hunter, roaming over large areas in search of the herds of grazing animals which were his main food. When these game animals were abundant man killed like a greedy glutton and some early camp sites have revealed huge pits of animal remains left by orgies of killing when game was plentiful. These leavings, which must have smelt abominably, possibly attracted packs of wolves and jackals to the camp sites. These members of the wild dog family, as well as hunting for themselves, will also act as scavengers, feeding from the dead carcases and carrion left by other killers. Packs of

Left: The coat of the Rough Collie is waterproof. It kept the dog warm and dry while working on the cold damp hills of Scotland, its native land. The colour here is tricolour.

wolves may have followed tribes of men whose wastefulness provided a supply of food for the bolder animals.

At first, both sides would have been very suspicious of each other but man probably also benefited from the presence of scavengers circling the outer darkness of his camp. Early men were not only hunters, they were also victims of larger, stronger predators. The behaviour of the wolves acted as a warning when these were near.

Perhaps the next step was taken when a litter of wolf cubs was found and reared by man. Some of these would have returned to the wild when they became adult but others might have

Top: The small, short muzzled toy dogs bred in China were meant to represent the mythical lion of Buddha. These little lion dogs are shown in many pottery pieces, like this early piece of porcelain. *Above:* This Egyptian mural shows an early type of greyhound. Throughout history, greyhounds have been bred for their speed as hunting animals.

stayed more or less permanently round the camps until at last men and wolves combined on hunting forays. Excavations in France have shown that, very early on, tribes of men and packs of wild dogs combined to panic herds of horses over the edge of cliffs, a method

Patterns of behaviour
The wild dog and the domestic dog share many patterns of instinctive behaviour and by watching one we may learn about the other.

Many dogs circle round before lying down. Possibly wild dogs trampled a bed in concealing vegetation this way.

Some breeds are much more aggressive than others and different breeds tend to have different fighting techniques.

Dogs rely more on facial expression and body posture to convey their intentions than they do on making sounds. Growling may be threatening or may be used in play and mock fights.

Marking scent posts with urine is part of the behaviour of a male dog. He indicates sex and status this way.

of hunting which provided more than enough meat for all. We now believe that the domesticated dog almost certainly descended from a wolf-like ancestor.

All the members of the wild dog family have a well developed sense of smell. Early tribes must have seen clearly the advantages of this when men and dogs combined to hunt together. From following behind to pick up the leavings, the dog went ahead to pick up the trail and, if necessary, hold at bay the wounded prey. Once the hunting dog could be relied upon to find hidden game by following a scent, the partnership of man and dog was well established.

Putting the dog to work
It did not take man very long to find other uses for the dog. Undoubtedly the dog was eaten when times were hard. It is still eaten in some parts of the world today. The animal's skin and fur would also be useful as clothing. Until quite recently many gloves were made of dog skin, and combings of dog hair can be spun and knitted by those who like to take the trouble. Early man used the dog as a source of warmth too, benefiting from the fact that the dog has a slightly higher temperature than our own. The domestic pet asleep on someone's bed

Left: A breed not yet widely recognized is the Pharaoh Hound, a very lithe, agile hunting dog from the Mediterranean area. The short, glossy coat is always chestnut or rich tan. A white tail-tip and toes are permissible. *Right:* The Pekingese is one of the most popular of the toy dogs. Its admirers stress its character, courage and dignity. The coat can be any colour.

has a long tradition behind it as a human bedwarmer.

From being solely a hunter, man progressed to being a herdsman, first of reindeer and later of cattle and sheep. These provided not only food and clothing but also wealth. The dog became a guard to warn off thieves and protect the cattle and sheep from their enemies, including the dog's own ancestor, the wolf. Probably man was still nomadic and the dog helped to move the flocks and herds along the tribes' annual migratory routes.

We know little about the appearance of these dogs but they probably resembled the Spitz – that is they had pricked ears, thick body fur, a wedge-shaped head and a bushy tail curled over the back. Spitz breeds are found world-wide today from the sledge dogs of the far north to the bear-hunting Akita of Japan, from the Norwegian Elkhound to the tiny toy Pomeranian. When the huts of the lake-dwelling peoples of Switzerland were excavated by modern archaeologists, it was the bones of this type of dog that they found.

Dogs of Ancient Egypt

The drawings of the cave dwellers show men and dogs hunting elk and horses. However the pictures are too crude and indistinct for us to guess the kind of dog these early hunters used. It is not until we get to the time of the Ancient Egyptians that we can see, from wall and tomb paintings, that already a number of different kinds of dog were being bred. One of these dogs was smooth-coated with a tail curled tightly over its back, very like the modern Basenji. Perhaps the most interesting dogs shown are the greyhounds, of which by 2000 BC there were already several varieties. All had the stream-lined shape of dogs who catch their prey by having enough speed to overtake it quickly. Some looked rather like our modern greyhounds but there were others with smooth coats and big upright ears, very like the Pharaoh hound of today. Yet others have the same soft, silky feathering on their legs and tails that distinguish the modern Saluki. Also shown in these early pictures are dogs with coat patterns spotted and marbled with different colours and also short-legged dogs like the Basset and Dachshund.

The Ancient Egyptians were very skilled animal breeders indeed. They kept in semi-domestication a number of species of animal that are considered today to be completely wild. Though they bred dogs for special tasks, such as hunting the desert gazelle, they also liked dogs just as companions as we do today.

Some of the excavated Egyptian tombs have contained the mummified remains of very tiny dogs. These little dogs wore jewelled collars and were buried with their owners so that they might accompany them in the spirit world.

Egypt's war-like neighbours, the Assyrians, were famous for their mastiffs, which are shown, carved in stone, going out with their masters to hunt lions. These dogs were massively built and were big enough to come up to the waist height of the men leading them. They wore collars made of a metal spiral round their necks so that when the prey was sighted their leashes could be quickly slipped off. Not only did they take part in lion hunts they also went to war beside their masters. These animals were so courageous that they were famed throughout the entire Mediterranian region.

Certainly by the year 2000 BC the civilizations of the Middle East were breeding a number of different types of hunting dog, some of which appear to have survived almost unchanged until the present day. We know more about these dogs than we do of those in other parts of the world. This is because such dogs were shown on wall paintings, carved friezes, papyrus scrolls and decorated pottery, some of which still survive as treasured museum exhibits.

The peoples of the Far East were also skilled dog breeders, particularly of small breeds with flattened muzzles, of which the best example is the Pekingese. Dogs of this type were bred in the Imperial Palace at Peking in China for many centuries before they ever reached the western world.

Early dogs in North America

We know very little of early American dogs because there is very little in the way of historical record. Dogs certainly played an important part in the life of some of the American Indian tribes. Many legendary stories are told of them and they have important roles in some Indian myths. Dance masks of carved and painted wood show both dogs and wolves.

Dogs were certainly kept for food and also used as pack animals, pulling the wooden travois. This was a rack-like arrangement made of poles lashed together, on to which household goods could be loaded and which could be dragged along either by dogs or ponies. We do not know for certain what these dogs looked like but it is thought that they may have been of the Spitz type.

Further south, in pre-Columbian Mexico, the Aztec peoples were breeding small dogs which played important roles in their religious ceremonies. Some people think that these little animals might be the ancestors of the Chihuahua but this is by no means certain. A terracotta model from Mexico dated about AD 300 shows a very fat little beast for, though cherished and pampered in their lives, these dogs were deliberately fattened so that they could be eaten.

Man and dog – social animals

Obviously the man and dog partnership has been a very successful one all over the world. Some of the reasons for this are easy to understand but some require a little more thought. First of all, the dog, like man, is a very adaptable creature. It

Left: Young puppies very often do not resemble the adult animal. This is a five-week-old German Shepherd. The drop ears will become erect as the dog gets older. The soft puppy coat will lighten in colour and coarsen in texture. *Right:* These Salukis are half grown and at the gawky, clumsy stage when it seems difficult to imagine that they will ever become graceful adults. *Below:* The bulk of the old English Mastiff makes it an unsuitable companion for anyone with a small living space. They are, however, a breed with a long and romantic history behind them.

How dogs communicate

To work together like this dogs must be able to communicate with each other. Human beings rely on speech but dogs rely on facial expressions, ear and tail carriage, and body posture. Watching dogs carefully can tell you a great deal about how they are feeling and what they are likely to do next. The aggressive dog is stiff and tense in its attitude. The head is held high and the eyes have a fixed glare. The hair along the spine stands on end making the dog seem larger and more powerful. Such an animal will circle its opponent with a stiff stilted walk. The muzzle will be drawn back to show a formidable row of teeth and this threat may be accompanied by growling and snarling.

On the other hand the nervous dog gives the impression of being smaller than it is. The ears are laid back and the body is held in a crouching attitude. The dog may even crawl on its belly. The tail is held tightly between the legs and such an animal will always keep its head towards the threatened danger. If it cannot run away, the nervous dog will be forced into threatening attitudes and will bite through fear.

Confident dogs have a relaxed and jaunty air. Their tails will be held high and they will neither slink nor stalk stiff-legged towards another dog. Play amongst puppies very often imitates the behaviour they will use as adults. The mock fighting which occurs in a litter serves to sort out which animals will be the dominant pack members and which will be the rank and file. Without this opportunity to test out his brothers and sisters in play while they are puppies a dog may be a life-long bully or a coward.

Using dogs' instincts

Man has used the wild instincts of the dog in order to create breeds better adapted for his purposes. To a dog, the most important of its senses is the sense of smell. By using it, the dog can find things which man using mere eyesight cannot. So dogs not only hunt for man, using their noses to follow a scent, they also detect for man, using their noses to find the hidden thief in the warehouse or the smuggled drugs in someone's luggage. There is no limit to man's ingenuity in using the dog's superior sense of smell. Dogs were used in wartime to clear paths through minefields for they could both scent and indicate the position of the mines.

The wild dog will make a kill, eat its fill, and then carry the rest off to its mate and cubs, or simply to bury it elsewhere. Man has utilized this instinct in the retrieving breeds, the bird dogs who seek

Young animals spend a great deal of time playing, as these two wolves are doing. Mock fighting and wrestling develops muscular co-ordination, and stalking and catching a litter mate is good practice for later hunting techniques.

can live in a wide variety of climates and is not too fussy about the food it eats. One of the reasons why both the Muslims and the Hebrews regard the dog as unclean is because it is a scavenger, feeding on carrion and rotting flesh. There are still many packs of pariah dogs in the world today, homeless animals roaming the streets and feeding off the waste of the big cities.

As well as being adaptable, the dog also resembles man in being a social animal. This means it does not live alone in the wild but in a pack with others of its own kind. The pack instinct is very important even to today's pet dog. A dog needs company if it is to be a contented animal and it is quite happy to accept its owner and its owner's family as a substitute pack to which it can belong. It is a form of cruelty to keep a dog shut up or chained up on its own for long periods of time. Dogs treated like this become bored, destructive and noisy. Families where everyone is at work or school all day should consider keeping a different sort of pet. The cat, being a solitary creature in the wild, does not suffer in the same way if left alone

to fend for itself for long periods day after day.

All social animals, whether they live in herds, flocks or packs, tend to have a leader who is recognized and respected by all the other members of the group. This lead animal is obeyed by the others and enforces a sort of rough justice. This prevents unnecessary fighting which would weaken the group as a whole. Within the pack there tends to be a ranking order right down to the bottom dog who can be bullied by everyone without making any protest. The pack leader is usually the strongest male, but it is not only physical strength that counts, it is also force of personality. The pet dog, like its wild relatives, needs a pack leader whom it can respect and obey and this is one of the reasons why it is important to train your dog. By doing so you make sure that the dog understands that you are boss and it will be happy to follow your lead.

A pack of dogs is capable of working together to a common end, such as pulling down and killing an animal much larger than could be tackled by one dog alone. This is one of the dangers of allowing your dog to roam. It may very well meet up with others to form a destructive group. Many people who were convinced that their dog would never harm other people's livestock, have been horrified to find that their pet could be a ruthless hunter when running with other dogs.

out and bring back to hand the dead or wounded game. To the retrievers, fetching and carrying comes easily, but most other breeds can be taught this and it is considered an essential in the training of police, army and guide dogs. Dogs also have an instinct to guard their own territory. Many a family pet, as part of a human pack, will be prepared to defend its master's property as its own.

Right: The brilliant red colouring of the Finnish Spitz makes it very distinctive. As well as general purpose farm dogs they are used as bird dogs in Finland.
Below: The huskies are the work horses of the frozen north. Without them the Eskimo could not have survived nor the Arctic have been explored.

Chapter two
Sporting Dogs

The Ancient Egyptians bred swift dogs to hunt the desert gazelle. Assyrian mastiffs helped their masters hunt lions. In medieval times dogs helped in the sport of falconry. Today dogs still take part in the sporting scene, and a highly trained pointer or retriever at work is a joy to watch.

Sporting dogs are those breeds which have been developed specifically to help man catch and kill other animals. Man and dog hunting together is an age-old partnership and the two have combined to catch every kind of prey from lion down to quail. Sporting dogs can be divided into three groups – the gundogs, the hounds and the terriers. There are some sixty or so different breeds in these categories recognized by the kennel clubs of Britain and America.

Gundogs

Some of the present day breeds of gundog can trace their descent from the hunting dogs used in medieval times for the sport of falconry. Hawking was one of the favourite pastimes throughout Europe from the ninth century onwards until the development of sporting guns. Dogs were employed to find and flush the game for the waiting hawks circling overhead. The word 'flush' means that, having found the scent of game, the dog creeps forward until the prey loses its nerve and either bolts from cover or flies upward presenting a target for the falconer or today's sportsman with a gun.

Writers of the 15th and 16th centuries tell us of the use of 'spaniels' and though we have no very clear idea of the looks of these dogs, their constantly wagging tail was even then, a note-worthy feature of the spaniel type. Springing spaniels found birds like the partridge and the quail and flushed them so that the falcons had a chance of an aerial chase. Setting spaniels also used their noses to find the coveys but, instead of flushing the birds, they showed they had found game by freezing into position with head held low, one forefoot raised and tail

The Borzoi was often known as the Russian Wolfhound. In Czarist Russia these dogs were kept by the aristocracy and used for coursing wolves. Borzois remain symbols of luxury today.

rigidly held out behind. The aim was to try and pin the birds to the ground long enough for a moveable net to be drawn over both birds and dog. In the work of the springing spaniel we can see the forerunners of the present day spaniel breeds. The setting spaniels foreshadow the setters and pointers of today. These dogs locate their quarry by windborne scent and freeze into the classical pose of a pointing dog indicating the position of the birds and trying to keep them pinned down until the arrival of the guns. Pointers and setters are, therefore, lightly built dogs of great stamina, for their work requires them to quarter the ground at a gallop ranging far ahead of the line of guns.

Retrieving

As sporting guns improved, their increased velocity meant that birds flying high overhead often fell a long way ahead of the sportsman. This led to the development of the retrieving breeds whose job was to find and fetch back dead and wounded game. As injured birds will run great distances, retrievers had to have good noses so that they could track down the birds. They also had to have tender mouths so that they could carry birds back without mangling the corpses.

Spaniels also find and flush game but they work much closer to the sportsman and are particularly useful for hunting through undergrowth or searching fields of root crops. They are also expected to retrieve whatever has been shot. Finally, there are a group of all-purpose gundog breeds, mostly continental in origin, who find and point birds, flush them on command and retrieve them when they have been shot.

There is a great deal of public interest in the work of gundogs and in gundog training. Field trials, in which the work of the dogs is tested competitively, are held. However, because of the enthusiasm shown and the numbers involved, many

The English Springer Spaniel is an active gundog which makes an energetic companion animal. The colouring is usually liver and white. This is one of the oldest of the several spaniel breeds.

of the conditions are artificial.

Dogs bred for sporting purposes, as shooting companions or field trial competitors, have more attention paid to their working abilities than they do to their looks. With show dogs it is the other way round, the build and the appearance of the animal are what counts and no attempt is made to see if it can still do the job for which it was originally bred. This has led to different types within the same breed. A field trial dog will stand no chance in the show ring and a show dog is unlikely to do well in working conditions. If you choose one of the gundog breeds as a companion dog it is probably better to get one from a show strain. If you want to work your dog, choose from a kennel whose dogs are used in the field. It is not fair to choose a dog from working stock, one whose very being is tied up with the delights of using its nose to hunt, and keeping such an animal as a pet with no scope to use its inbred abilities. Such dogs can become neurotic and destructive with frustration.

Gundog breeds

Gundogs as companions are very active, and usually responsive to any kind of training. Among the setters, the Irish is probably the most popular, a big rangy, mahogany red dog, often boisterous, fun-loving and headstrong. As with most Irish breeds, there is little known about the breed's history but their flamboyant colouring and matching personality have made them popular pets. Few, if any, are working gundogs today in contrast to the English Setter where field as well as show strains exist. The white background of the English Setter's silky coat is softly flecked and freckled with either blue, orange or in some cases lemon markings.

We can trace the history of the Pointer back to the 17th century. As a bird dog this breed has few equals for the sportsman who has a lot of open country to hunt. It is short-coated, muscular and full of that nervous energy which provides the drive for the active hunting animal.

The soulful look of the Basset Hound has deceived many into thinking that it is a staid and stolid dog. In fact it is energetic and determined, with a zest for life.

Pointers and setters were the only dogs scheduled at the first dog show held in Britain in 1859 and it was only these sporting breeds that appeared at the first American show in 1874. What is more, the first dog registered with the American Kennel Club was an English Setter. However, in today's order of popularity it would be the retrievers who top the bill with both the Labrador and the Golden Retriever being widely kept. Both these dogs can still work with the gun but their kindly natures and willingness to please have made them firm favourites as companion animals. Their responsiveness to training means that they are also used as drug detection

Hunting in the United States
The dog's sense of smell is infinitely superior to ours. This is one of the reasons why the hunting partnership between people and dogs has been so successful for so long. These pictures show the game hunted in the United States, and the dogs which do the hunting.

Basset hound   snowshoe rabbit

Pointer   bobwhite quail

racoon   Coonhound

American foxhound   American red fox

Right: Like the Basset, the Dachshund is another low-to-ground animal with a good nose for following a scent. The short legs and long flexible body allow this dog to go underground after its quarry, the badger, with ease. Most Dachshunds love comfort and adapt very well to town life. *Right below:* Foxhound puppies like these grow up used to pack life and pack discipline. They are not satisfactory as pets.

dogs, police dogs and guide dogs for the blind. Both these breeds are powerfully built with excellent noses and they both have a fondness for water.

Labradors, which originally came from Newfoundland and not the Labrador coast, can be black or yellow (and, more rarely, chocolate) in colour. They have smooth, thick, water-resistant coats. The Golden Retriever's coat is wavy and moderately long and can be any shade from cream through to tawny.

Among the spaniels, Cockers are the most popular of pets, being friendly, merry dogs which come in a wide variety of coat colours. They are no longer expected to work with the gun unlike the English Springer Spaniel, which is still a versatile breed and very popular because of it.

The Brittany spaniel is also a very popular working gundog, a long-legged spaniel expected to 'point' like a setter when scenting game. This dog is an all-round gundog rather than a specialist and the orange and white colouring is a breed characteristic.

Another all-round gundog, expected to hunt, point, flush and retrieve game is the German Short-haired Pointer which is again a very popular dog with the shooting man. It makes an energetic but biddable pet for those who have the time and space to exercise such a dog. The short, harsh coat is usually ticked liver and white.

Scent-hounds

The hound breeds can be divided into two groups; the dogs which hunt by scent and the dogs which hunt by sight. The scent hounds include such breeds as Foxhounds, Beagles, Bassets, Coonhounds, Bloodhounds and the more unusual Elkhound, Basenji and Dachshund. Most of these dogs usually hunt in packs and accounts of man hunting with packs of hounds go back to our earliest historical records. Scent hounds are not necessarily very fast. What they do possess is tenacity of purpose which keeps them following a scent relentlessly, wearing down their game by their persistence rather than overtaking it with superior speed.

The Ancient Greeks used hounds to hunt deer, wolves, wild boar and hares, and since then hounds have been used in many different ways in many different countries. In some parts of the world hounds are trained to work round behind game and drive it towards the guns. Other sportsmen have expected their hounds both to find and retrieve game that has been shot.

The greatest variety of hound breeds was probably developed in France where hunting was considered an art by the nobility and every château had its own distinctive pack of hounds. Many of these did not survive the French Revolution for republican anger was not only directed against the nobility but also against the way of life which included such extravagances as personal packs of hounds. The unfortunate dogs perished with their masters.

By far the greatest number of hounds in the modern world is in the United States, where there are reckoned to be well over one and a half million. Unlike the English Foxhound which is always a pack animal kept for fox-hunting alone, the American Foxhound can be used in a variety of ways and for this reason is not very uniform in type. Although the American red fox is sometimes hunted by packs of hounds who are followed on horseback, it is also hunted by a sportsman with a gun who needs a slow-trailing hound with a good voice. Drag hounds, which race along a specially laid trail, need speed and stamina alone while the field trail hound needs speed and a rather jealous nature if it is to compete effectively.

Hound music
All the scent hounds give tongue or bay when following a scent and this hound music tells the huntsman both where the dogs are and also how near they are to their quarry. Nowhere is this more important than with the coonhounds, of which there are six varieties, though only one, the Black-and-Tan Coonhound, is recognized by the American Kennel Club. Coon hunting is a very popular sport in some of the southern states of America and, where it is run on a competitive basis, marks are given for the quality of the hound music as the dog bays the scent of the treed racoon.

As a pet dog the most popular hound is the Beagle, a merry little dog with a smart-as-paint exterior. Undoubtedly an old European breed, the Beagle has been used as a pack hound to hunt the hare for centuries and European-type Beagles were first imported into the United States by eminent sportsmen in the 1870s and 1880s. Since then, many people have kept a few Beagles for their own sporting pleasure, and many more have been kept as pets by people who liked their sporting character and their handy size.

The Basset Hound is another pack hound that has become a family favourite. Slow, short-legged, hounds like these are French in origin and next to the Bloodhound, are the breed credited with the best scenting powers and the sweetest of hound music. Most Bassets have kindly natures but many an owner has been deceived by those short legs into thinking that they are small dogs. In fact, though low to ground, they are quite large dogs, and their somewhat lugubrious expression hides a rollicking hearty appetite for both food and exercise.

All hounds that have lived cheek by jowl with others of their kind for centuries tend to be non-aggressive. They do, however, like company and will roam both to be sociable and also to follow the intriguing scents that have been their chief interest for so long in their history.

The most famous of the hounds that hunt by scent, though it has never been the one most widely kept, is the Bloodhound. The deeply wrinkled forehead, heavy jowls and long drooping ears give the breed the most melancholy of expressions but also serve to hide the most sensitive nose in the business. In their long history they have been used to hunt runaway slaves, find missing persons and track down wanted criminals. The rather spine-chilling name actually means pure-blooded for these dogs have been known and valued for a thousand years. Today's hound is rather a gentle, kindly beast with a sensitive nature but still with that amazing tenacity on a cold scent, and the most sonorous and unforgettable of hound music while hunting a line. Bloodhound enthusiasts run working trials to test their hound's scenting abilities. Contrary to popular belief, these hounds are rarely ferocious even towards those animals that they have been tracking.

Deerhounds seem to have changed very little in either appearance or character over the centuries. They have great power and grace when hunting.

Sight-hounds

The hounds which hunt by sight are sometimes called gaze- or wind-hounds. These breeds are all built for speed so that they can overtake the swiftest and most agile of quarry. Their shape is streamlined with no superfluous flesh or fat, and the rib-cage is deep to allow plenty of heart and lung room. The back is strong and flexible so that it acts as a powerful spring, bending and straightening as the dog gallops. The limbs are long and powerful and so is the tail which acts as an efficient rudder so that the dog can turn and twist at speed. These dogs run mute, needing all their breath for galloping. They are only

Left: The Poodle was originally a gundog and can still give a good account of itself in the field. The Standard size, as shown here, makes a powerful swimmer and a good wildfowl dog. The all-over clip keeps the coat a manageable length. *Below:* The Afghan Hound was introduced to the western world by British army officers who brought them back from their native Afghanistan at the turn of the century.

suitable for hunting game in open country since, once their quarry is out of sight, they take no further interest in it.

The thrill of coursing live game across open country has been replaced for town dwellers by the thrills of greyhound racing. Few greyhounds are kept as show or companion animals compared with the very large numbers that are registered with the governing bodies of the greyhound racing world. Greyhounds are probably the fastest of the running dogs, though Saluki enthusiasts might dispute this.

The Saluki was bred to chase the desert gazelle across the burning sands of Arabia and dogs of this type seem to have existed for at least four thousand years. Like many of the gaze-hounds, Salukis are now kept solely as pets and show dogs by people who admire their elegance and grace. Perhaps the most fashionable of the sight-hounds today is the Afghan, a dog designed to travel at top speed over rough terrain. The long, silky coat is one of the glories of the breed but grooming such a dog is a time-consuming daily chore.

Gundogs are no use to the sportsman unless they are fully trained and responsive to his command. Hounds hunt on their own initiative and the hunter follows where they lead. They should not give up too easily and must be deaf to distractions when they are following a line. Hounds therefore tend to have independent, even obstinate, natures and, together with the third group of sporting dogs, the terriers, are the least easily trained of breeds.

Terriers

The terriers are the vermin killers of the world. They were bred to tackle anything from rats to polecats and foxes. What is

Above: The work of a pointer is to gallop ahead of the hunter, quartering the ground with head up to catch the air scent of hidden coveys of birds. Once these have been located the dog should freeze to indicate their position. This dog is making a rather tentative point. The lack of tense expectation suggests that the animal is not sure of its find. *Left:* Labradors, being strong swimmers, make good wildfowler's dogs.

more they were expected to face their enemies underground, to bolt the fox from his earth or dig out the rat cornered under the stack. They are therefore dogs with tremendous courage for their size. Some can be too aggressive for their owner's peace of mind and many have coats which require a great deal of expert trimming if the dog is not to look like an untidy doormat. Terriers by definition are smart, peppy dogs and a dowdy or nervous terrier is very unusual.

Most of the terrier breeds come from Britain and they were often dogs from a very localized area. This is shown by the breed names which are often those of places – Airedale, Border, Sealyham and Bedlington for example. Scotland, a country where many breeds originated, has the distinction of being the home of a number of the short-legged terrier breeds. Among the most popular are the Scottish Terrier and the Cairn Terrier. Both these and the West Highland White Terrier were bred to weasel their way into the cracks and crannies which housed their enemies, the wild cat, the marten and the rat. To deal with these at close quarters the dogs had to have unlimited courage, strong jaws and teeth

Left: The Brittany Spaniel is one of the most popular of working gundogs. Its small size and short coat compared with some of the other gundogs, help to make it an excellent house dog as well as a first class sporting companion. The colour must be either dark orange and white or liver and white. *Below:* A Golden Retriever does the job it was bred for, fetching back a dead duck which fell out of reach of the sportsman.

Left: The Irish Setter is today so universally known for its mahogany coat that it is nicknamed the Red Setter.

and a waterproof jacket of a coat that would protect them from the cold, damp climate of their native land.

Scotties are dogs of great personality, very loyal to their friends but a bit dour with strangers. The coat is usually black and needs a lot of trimming to keep it smart. The Westie also needs some trimming but the short, harsh coat does not pick up the dirt as quickly as one might suspect and it is therefore comparatively easy to keep this white dog clean. The Cairn Terrier, like its jaunty cousin the Westie, is a cheeky little dog with a cheerful disposition. The shaggy coat needs little in the way of attention and can be any shade of grey, wheaten or brindle.

The longer-legged terriers like the Welsh, Lakeland and Fox Terrier, often ran with the foxhounds and came into their own when the fox went to earth. Fox Terriers can either be wire-haired or smooth-haired. A number of other terrier breeds were developed for the cruel practice of organized dog fighting. These include the Staffordshire Terrier and the English Bull Terrier. Oddly enough many of the fighting breeds are very sweet tempered towards the human race. However, they do need training.

Irish terriers
Like Scotland, Ireland is also the home of a number of terrier breeds. But their history, like that of most Irish breeds, is not very well documented. The Irish Terrier is an exuberant and inquisitive dog, a typical specimen of the long-legged terrier clan with a wire-haired coat which must be red in colour. Held in amused esteem by his friends, and not a little respect by his canine enemies, the Irish Terrier has gained a number of nicknames of which 'the Red Devil' is one example.

The Kerry Blue Terrier also comes from Ireland. It is one of the larger terriers and looks more bulky than it really is because of its wavy, soft and very plentiful coat. This is sculpted with scissors to give the dog the smart outline that is necessary for the show ring, and the result looks rather like a dog in an astrakhan coat. The colour must be blue, though puppies are born black and the coat lightens to the required shade. The soft-coated Wheaten Terrier is another with a silky, soft coat. Used as general farm dogs and for driving cattle, it looks very much like that other small herding dog, the Tibetan Terrier, whose duties were much the same.

The breeding of foxhounds has been carefully controlled and recorded since the 18th century. Within most packs type is very uniform and the individuals differ little in conformation from each other. However, there are often marked differences between packs, due of course to the fact that different packs hunt different types of country. The hounds shown above hunt hill foxes.

Chapter three
Working Dogs

When people first became herdsmen, they used dogs to guard their flocks and possessions. Today dogs still herd sheep and cattle, and guard houses. They also guide the blind, sniff out illegal drugs, track down criminals, rescue climbers in difficulty, pull sledges and even star in films.

Today probably more dogs are kept as companion animals than for any other single reason, but this is a very recent development. In the past the dog has nearly always been a working animal, whose worth was gauged by its usefulness. Many of the useful jobs that dogs did have been taken over by machines. Roasting meat is no longer turned on a spit by a little dog running inside a wheel. We have a powered motor to do the job instead, and the kind of dog which did this, called a turnspit, no longer exists. Machines, therefore, have not only taken over many of the jobs once done by people, but also many of those done by dogs. Oddly enough, though, the dog's usefulness does not seem to diminish. The kind of work differs now – modern dogs may be trained as film stars, may be rocketed into space or may search cargoes for smuggled drugs – but we always seem to think of new tasks for our adaptable old friend.

Herding dogs
Men and dogs first joined together as hunting partners. The next stage in the development of early tribesmen was when they became nomadic herdsmen. Reindeer were probably the first animals to be kept for their meat, hides and milk. Man now had possessions to be guarded and the dog was expected to keep the flocks and herds safe from such predators as wolves. They must also have been a great deterrent against thieves. Obviously dogs for such

purposes had to be large and powerful. They were expected to act on their own initiative and were often left on their own to guard the flocks.

These herding dogs sometimes had their necks protected by collars with long metal spikes which prevented the wolf getting a grip on the dog's throat, and they also often had their ears cropped – that is the ear flap was cut off. This too was a protective measure since the ear bleeds very freely and, with little of the ear flap left, opponents had less chance of gripping and tearing. From being a protective measure, there grew the superstitious belief that chopping a dog's ears off actually made it a more courageous animal. Today this

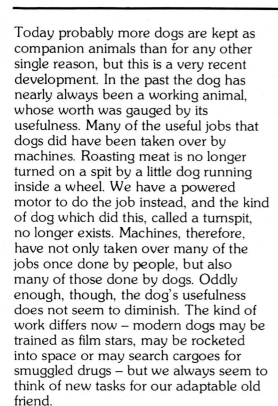

Above: Much of the charm of the Tibetan Terrier lies in its unkempt and ragamuffin appearance. Little known here, they were the watchdogs and the herdsman's dogs of Tibet.

somewhat barbarous practice is still continued in the name of fashion, and some breeds are cropped because it is supposed to make them look smarter.

A surprising number of these big herdsman's guard dogs were white in colour, perhaps so that they could easily be distinguished from the wolf when it came to a fight in defence of the flock. Among the two best known today are the Great Pyrenees, or Pyrenean Mountain Dogs, from France and the

Left: The keen eyesight of the greyhound will focus on the slightest flicker of movement in the distance. Their traditional quarry, the hare, will 'freeze' into immobility, well knowing that absolute stillness means safety, since greyhounds rarely use their noses to hunt. *Right:* The Komondor is a guard dog for the flocks and herds which roam the vast Hungarian plains.

Komondor from the plains of Hungary. The Komondor is still a working dog in Hungary where it lives a semi-nomadic existence looking after flocks of long-legged and very active native sheep. This dog has one of the most extraordinary of coats, the entire body being covered with long, soft, woolly white hair. On the working dog this felts and mats into a solid fleece which can be long enough to drag on the ground and provides almost total protection against the weather and any injury. Of course it also gets extremely dirty and provides an impenetrable haven for fleas and lice, which is possibly why the Komondor is strictly an outdoor dog in Hungary. The few which are shown in the United States and, in Britain have their long coats twisted into cords.

The modern sheepdog

Sheepdogs are now rarely called upon to act as guards and therefore tend to be smaller dogs, lithe, muscular and with the stamina to work long hours, galloping across rough country to gather in widely scattered sheep. There are a number of different types of working sheepdogs but the two most widely used throughout the world are the Australian Kelpie and the British Border Collie. Many of the breeds which people think of as sheepdogs are no longer capable of doing the work for which they were originally bred. Among these are the Rough Collie and the Old English Sheepdog. The Rough Collie came from Scotland where it had been a working farm dog for centuries. The breed became fashionable in the 19th century when Queen Victoria, who was a great dog lover, added some to her kennels. The new sport of dog showing helped to fan the enthusiasm for the breed. It began to be 'improved' by exhibitors who wanted a narrower, more refined head and a more glamorous coat than was carried by the breed's working forefathers. The Rough Collie has remained popular from that day to this, particularly helped by the publicity from the films starring Lassie. Lassie in fact was rather a fraud, being a dog not a bitch, but so popular was this canine film star that Rough Collies are often called Lassie dogs.

The Old English Sheepdog is a member of the family of shaggy sheepdogs, examples of which can be found in nearly every European country. The French have the Briard, the Spanish have the Catalan sheepdog, and other shaggy sheepdog breeds are found in Holland, Poland and Russia. Britain has two, the Bearded Collie and the Old English Sheepdog, breeds which are

believed to have shared a common ancestor. The Old English has the nick-name of Bobtail because its tail has always been cut off very short. This helps give the dog rather a cumbersome appearance, the shaggy coat and rounded rump making it look rather bear-like in shape. However these big, bouncy dogs are surprisingly agile and fast when they want to be. Their ancestors drove cattle and ponies to market in the south of England but the Bobtail has left its working past a long way behind. Any dog as heavily coated as this breed needs a good deal of time spent on daily grooming.

The best known cattle dog from France is the Briard, a dark coloured dog with a long wavy coat which effectively hides a powerful and muscular body. The Briard is one of those oddities, like the Great Pyrenees, whose breed standard requires it to have double dew claws on each hind leg. Absence of this feature brings disqualification in the show ring.

The Belgian Sheepdog is one of four closely related breeds all of which bear a certain resemblance to the German Shepherd, and it is possible that all these breeds stemmed from the same root.

Above: Underneath the incredible coat, the Hungarian Puli is a nimble, active and brainy dog. However, the length and density of its corded hair make it difficult to keep clean.

The Belgian Sheepdog is a very square animal in outline and is always black in colour. Like many of the shepherding breeds it has a jealous and possessive nature. This is balanced by a complete devotion to its master and a strong desire to please. Typically the Belgian Sheepdog is reserved with strangers.

The German Shepherd

As the name suggests the German Shepherd, or Alsatian, as it is known in Britain, was also bred as a sheepdog. This breed is probably the best known and most popular dog in the world. Few people are indifferent to these dogs. To a devoted band of owners the breed is supreme both in looks and temperament. Yet to others it is a dog to be regarded with suspicion, an unreliable animal whose savagery has made newspaper headlines. One of the reasons for this dual attitude is that the breed is a very popular one.

Left: The Old English Sheepdog was once used for driving cattle and ponies to market and, despite a rather clumsy appearance, is still an active and agile dog with a fair turn of speed.

Unfortunately in any breed that becomes very popular, temperament is liable to suffer. The demand for puppies is so great that unsuitable animals are used as breeding stock and dogs unreliable and nervous in character as well as poor in conformation, give the breed a bad name. It is sensible when getting any dog, to buy your puppy direct from a breeder who really cares about the future of your chosen breed. This advice is particularly true if you are going to buy a popular breed.

German Shepherds are not an old breed compared with many. The credit for the outstanding merits of this animal, which make it the most versatile of working dogs, goes to the German fanciers of some 80 or 90 years ago. They established the Shepherd as we know it today using local sheepdogs from the areas of Württemburg and Thuringia as their foundation stock. Sheepdogs in those areas were expected not only to protect their charges but also to prevent the flock straying among the crops grown on an unfenced strip system. The dogs were often left in sole charge and confined their sheep to the grazing areas by continually loping round

Dogs in Harness

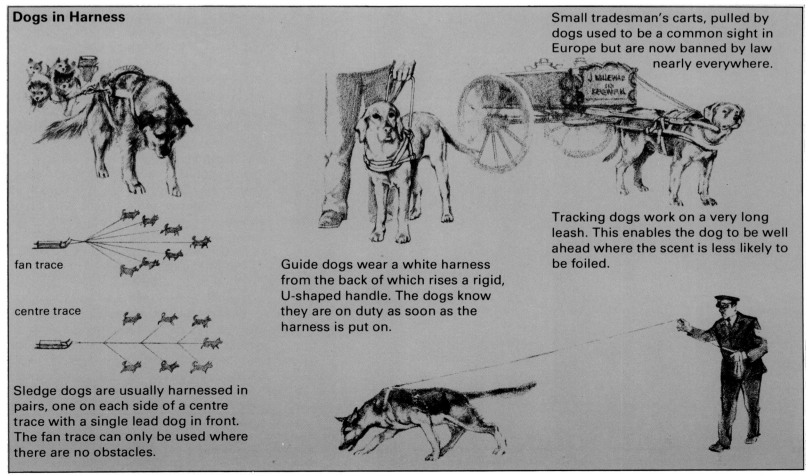

Small tradesman's carts, pulled by dogs used to be a common sight in Europe but are now banned by law nearly everywhere.

fan trace

centre trace

Sledge dogs are usually harnessed in pairs, one on each side of a centre trace with a single lead dog in front. The fan trace can only be used where there are no obstacles.

Guide dogs wear a white harness from the back of which rises a rigid, U-shaped handle. The dogs know they are on duty as soon as the harness is put on.

Tracking dogs work on a very long leash. This enables the dog to be well ahead where the scent is less likely to be foiled.

the flock. In other words the dogs had to be virtually tireless and able to act on their own initiative – both valuable attributes in a working animal. Today the dog is a strong and agile one with an effortless springy gait which enables it to cover a lot of ground with an economical stride. The coat is short but double, with a soft woolly undercoat and a weather resistant, harsh top coat. This kind of coat means that the dog can work in any climate for it acts as an insulation against both extreme heat and severe cold.

Unfortunate reputation

German breeders have always recognized that temperament is of equal importance to the conformation of a working dog and have paid great attention to it in their breeding programmes. Unfortunately this has not always been the case elsewhere. The breed was scarcely known outside its native land before the First World War. However, both the German army and the police used them on the battlefields as messenger dogs and as rescue dogs to find the wounded. They so impressed American and British soldiers that both took specimens of the breed home with them. In the 1920s the German Shepherd enjoyed an enormous success but as more and more dogs got into inexperienced ownership, mismanaged and bored animals displayed a destructive savagery that brought the breed into disrepute. They were labelled treacherous and their somewhat wolf-like

The German Shepherd is the best known and one of the most versatile of the working breeds. Their usefulness lies in their all-round ability in many fields. Other more specialized breeds are stronger, faster or as intelligent but few combine the talents of a good German Shepherd. The guard dog (below left) cannot be fully effective because of its chain. A well-trained dog will only attack if ordered and is a more efficient deterrent loose. *Below right:* This dog is being trained to attack on command. Like all training, this is done on the lead so that the dog is under its trainer's control. *Right:* Patient training can give an animal enough skill and confidence to overcome its instinctive fear of fire.

appearance was held against them. The numbers bred fell very sharply but organizations that needed reliable working dogs realized their value and, from that 1930 slump, the breed has slowly and steadily grown to be the premier working dog of the world.

A reliable working dog

As a police and army dog the German Shepherd's greatest value is as a deterrent. The presence of a trained dog discourages vandals and hooligans. Not only is the dog an added protection to the patrolman on his beat but the dog's scenting powers enable it to pick out much that its handler might miss. Dogs can be much more effective in searching a building than teams of men, and the threat of sending in the dogs has caused many a suspect to surrender. Given the right conditions a dog can wind a hidden stranger a hundred yards away. For this reason many frontier posts have dog patrols, and army units use dogs to warn of the approach of guerillas. They guard ammunition dumps and airfields and have been dropped by parachute into war zones. The breed has also served as a mine detector and as a First Aid dog, looking for wounded soldiers and civilians.

Their uses are not all military however. In mountainous country German Shepherds form the major part of the mountain rescue teams, those whose job it is to search for missing climbers. The dogs are trained to search, quartering the ground in the same way that police dogs are trained to search for hidden suspects. Avalanche rescue teams use dogs who can locate people buried under the snow and, by trying to dig down to them, alert their rescuers. In the same way a working sheepdog will show a shepherd where the blizzard has buried the flock so that he can dig them out.

The Doberman Pinscher

As a guard the German Shepherd is both protective and reliable but there are a number of other breeds that are equally effective as guard and police dogs. Foremost among these is the Doberman Pinscher. This too is a fairly modern breed dating only from about 1890. It was the creation of one man, Herr Dobermann, who wanted to breed a superlative guard dog. The Doberman Pinscher is one of the most lithe, muscular and alert dogs that it is possible to find. Its clean cut appearance and short glossy coat emphasize the

impression that this is a fearless dog, very quick to react. The breed quickly proved its worth as a police and army dog and is extensively used today. Herr Dobermann wanted a very sharp, fierce dog, a temperament that is not really suitable for anyone but a specialist trainer to own. Today the breed is still an excellent guard but is not quite so trigger happy as it used to be.

The story has it that one of the first Dobes imported into the United States had a very successful show career. Few judges were brave enough to handle the Doberman Pinschers then and it was

some considerable time before anyone was brave enough to open this particular dog's mouth and discover that, all along, it had the disqualifying fault of missing teeth.

Another German breed that makes a good guard dog, and is used both by the German police and army, is the Boxer. This is another solid muscular dog, very energetic and high-spirited. It is an animal that needs an active owner who is prepared to give it enough training to curb its boisterous enthusiasm. It is also smooth-coated, usually fawn or brindle with white markings.

and it is employed for both police and customs duties.

Diminutive watchdogs

A guard dog does not have to be large and brawny to be effective. Many smaller breeds are very efficient watchdogs being naturally alert and suspicious of the unusual. We have a number of modern breeds whose job in the past was mainly to warn of intruders on their master's property. One of these is the Lhasa Apso, a dog from Tibet with a long flowing coat and the arrogant expression common to many of the Far Eastern breeds. Though small in size they are very important dogs in their own estimation! One of their other Tibetan names means Bark Lion Sentinel Dog and they were bred as watchdogs for monasteries and the houses of rich merchants. The fierce Tibetan Mastiff guarded the outside while the little Lhasa Apso warned of intruders within the gates.

The Schipperke is another small guard dog, this time from Belgium. The name means 'little skipper' and these dogs often travelled on the canal boats of

Left: Like most of the Tibetan breeds, the Lhasa Apso carries a very heavy coat which helps to protect it in the extreme cold of its homeland. Golden or honey are the colours most prized. *Above:* As its name suggests, the Bull mastiff was created by crossing the more active bulldogs of the 19th century with the heavyweight mastiffs. The result was a guard dog of substance and power, a little too heavy for most police and army duties but an ideal protector of home and family. *Below:* The sinewy silhouette of the Doberman Pinscher shows the muscular power and alertness necessary for a police dog.

The head of the Boxer has the short muzzle and broad jaw of a dog descended from bull-baiting ancestors. Bull-baiting was a popular spectacle in Europe for a number of centuries. It was banned little more than 150 years ago. The tethered bull was maddened by having relays of dogs set upon it who tried to pin the bull by the nose. Bull-baiting dogs had to be courageous to the point of foolhardiness. They also had to grip and hang on while the wretched bull tried to free itself from torment by tossing and trampling on them.

The German police and army have always led the way in using trained dogs for patrol and guard duties. The necessity of guarding very long land frontiers possibly helped the Germans to realize the value of trained frontier patrol dogs. The Germans are also a people who have produced a number of very skilled animal trainers, and those in authority were not blind to the uses of dogs on the battlefield. One of the results of this is that the Germans make use of breeds which are often considered only as show dogs. A case in point is the Airedale Terrier. Comparable in size to the Boxer, but with the long muzzle and wiry coat typical of many of the terrier group, the Airedale is usually seen only as a well-barbered exhibition dog. In Europe however the breed is recognized as having the size, courage and intelligence needed for service training

Europe, watching the cargoes, warning of intruders and catching the odd rat or two. The coat is fairly short, but very dense and forms a big black ruff framing the pointed foxy face. Like all the guard dogs the Schipperke is a very loyal little dog to its friends and has a natural suspicion of strangers.

Dogs in harness

In the past many dogs were used as draught animals, that is they pulled carts or sledges for their masters, or carried packs strapped to their backs. In many European countries small tradesmen used dogs to pull carts full of their produce. Bread and milk would be delivered to customers this way, and such things as cheeses and vegetables would be taken to market. Most of these dogs were not purebred – any sizeable animal could be used. The Swiss, however, used the Bernese Mountain Dog quite extensively. This usage of dogs died out with the development of motor transport and is now banned.

Arctic sled dogs are, of course, the

Left: Guide dogs for the blind have one of the most responsible jobs that a dog can be trained to do. Here a yellow Labrador Retriever takes its blind owner to work. *Above:* Tradition has it that the St Bernard first found the snow-bound traveller and then revived him with brandy from the flask hung round the dog's neck. The dogs were used as pack animals by the monks and this probably gave rise to the myth. *Right:* The thin, supple skin of the Bloodhound is extremely loose, particularly about the head and neck, where the wrinkles give the dog a sad expression.

most famous of draught dogs. Without their dog teams the Eskimos of the frozen north could not have survived, nor could any of the early exploration of Polar areas have taken place. Sled dogs rely on the thickness of their coat to protect them in sub-zero temperatures. Staked out after a day's work, the dogs scraped a depression in the snow and curled up to sleep with their thick, bushy tail keeping their nose and feet protected against frostbite. Most working sled dogs were fed on frozen seal meat, a diet particularly rich in animal fats, which helped to maintain the density of coat necessary for the dog's survival.

The Arctic is a vast area and, since communications were always difficult, many isolated areas developed their own kind of sled dog. Three breeds recognized as purebred today are the Samoyed, Siberian Husky and Alaskan Malamute. Motorized transport has

replaced the husky in most areas but the sport of sled dog racing has now become a popular one and is held in most areas wherever there is enough snow. Speed is the most important thing in sled dog racing and these modern sled teams are not required to show the powers of endurance and the ability to pull heavy loads shown by the pioneers of the past. Drivers are always on the lookout for fast racing dogs and crossbreeds are commonly used in the sport.

Guide dogs for the blind

One of the modern uses for the dog has been in the development and training of guide dogs for the blind. This work was pioneered in Germany after 1918, when efforts were made to train dogs so that the many men blinded during the war could be helped. The Seeing Eye organization in the United States was founded by a Philadelphian woman, Mrs Harrison Eustis, who had watched the German experiments and set up her own

dog training school in Switzerland.

Guide dogs have the most responsible job that any dog can be called upon to do, for, in guiding their owners wherever they wish to go, the dog is responsible for the life and safety of its master. The selection and training of these animals is extremely rigorous and The Seeing Eye has its own breeding programme aimed at producing the right temperament for the job. Again German Shepherds are the most popular guide dogs.

Chapter four
Toy Dogs and Small Breeds

Small dogs have a lot to be said for them. They don't need a lot of space to live in, they don't need much exercise or eat much food. They provide companionship for a great many people.

For administrative convenience, the Kennel Clubs of America and Britain divide all the purebred dogs that they recognize into six groups. The Toy Group is the one which contains all the smallest breeds. It is perhaps rather unfortunately named as no living animal should be described as a toy nor should ever be treated as one. What is more, most toy dogs pack a personality plus into their small frame. Their sense of their own importance, their energy and their devotion to their human family are some of the merits which make small dogs irrestistible to those who have owned one.

The happiest of these dogs are those which live at the heart of the household, busily overseeing the family activities as part of their self-imposed duties and jealously guarding their own privileges and their owner's property. Because they are such close companions, many of these small dogs are able to size their owners up pretty accurately, and can be as demanding and selfish as spoilt children if allowed to have their own way too much. The over-indulgent owner, who over-feeds and under-exercises a dog is as guilty of cruelty as the owner who neglects an animal.

Advantages of a small dog

The advantages of a small dog are obvious. They fit neatly into any living space and life style. Their handy size means that they can go with their owners almost anywhere. They eat comparatively little, though because of their high energy output their food does need to be of high quality. Most of the smaller breeds are prepared to take as much or as little exercise as their owners feel inclined to give them, and the more

The miniature Wire-haired Dachshund is still very much a sporting dog who enjoys hunting and digging. It would be used in its native country, Germany, for burrowing after rabbits.

active types will still be dancing round their companions at the end of an hour-long walk.

Small dogs, correctly fed and exercised, present few health problems. Their size means that they are more susceptible to chills from cold and damp conditions. Obviously an accident such as a dog bite or being shut in a door is more serious for a tiny dog. However, the fear that many people have that they would step on so small a creature is unfounded. Toy dogs are much too active and sensible to allow that to happen. Some of the breeds with very flattened faces suffer from breathing troubles, and those with very prominent eyes are prone to eye injuries. However, breeds with these characteristics are not confined to the toys.

People are always interested in the exceptional and very tiny dogs that occasionally occur in Chihuahua, Yorkshire Terrier and Pomeranian litters. However the abnormally small are not usually as long-lived or hardy as the average sized animal in a breed and are therefore better avoided. Toy breeders quite often have puppies which they feel will grow too large for their purposes and these may be sold more cheaply and make excellent pets.

The popular Yorkie

Possibly the most popular of the toy breeds at the moment is the Yorkshire Terrier. A comparatively new breed, this dog was bred by the mill workers of the Yorkshire woollen towns and the miners of the coal pits. Looking at so fashionable a breed now it seems odd to think that they were created by working men who wanted a small spirited terrier for rat hunting. About 120 years ago the dogs were 12–15 lb (5·5–7 kg) in weight, but gradually the smaller type with the more glamorous coat was preferred. The Yorkie today averages about 5 lb (2·25 kg) in weight, and many show dogs are even smaller.

The Tibetan Spaniel is a gay and assertive little dog whose silken coat can be any colour. In the past they both acted as watchdogs for the Tibetan monks and turned the prayer wheels.

The coat of an exhibition Yorkie is its chief glory with colour, length and texture being important qualities. To keep the coat in good condition, so that it falls to floor level in a shining curtain of dark, steel blue and rich tan, is an art in itself. The hair is fine and silky and has to be oiled and rolled up in paper and ribbons to avoid damage. Though this leads to certain restrictions, most dogs enjoy the fuss and attention necessary to keep the glamour of their coat.

As a pet, the Yorkie is a very sensible shape and has the spirited determination of its terrier ancestors. The coat will be easier to manage if it is slightly shortened. The topknot of a show Yorkie is tied back with ribbon but a pet can have this cut to a fringe which leaves the dark, sparkling eyes showing.

The Pekingese

Many toy breeds have romantic histories, and not the least of these is the Pekingese. The breed can be traced back to the 8th century and may very well be even older than that. They were Imperial dogs raised in the old Manchu Palace in Peking to be the particular favourites of the Emperor and his court. They were bred with the greatest care, and the finest dogs were painted on the scrolls kept in the Imperial Palace as a kind of breed record. The most desirable points were the flat face with large, luminous eyes, the small size and the heavy coat, and the dignity and courage of a lion. All colours were bred and markings had symbolic meanings. The first Pekingese to reach the West were four which were looted by British troops who sacked the Summer Palace in Peking. The year was 1860. One of the dogs was given to Queen Victoria, so

Left: Smooth-coat Chihuahuas have a soft, close, glossy coat which can be any colour. The skull, rounded like an apple, and the large ears give this tiny dog a saucy expression.

moving from an Eastern royal residence to a Western one. Here it remained one of the Queen's favourites for the next twelve years. The other three were the foundation stock for the 'Goodwood' kennel. From these dogs and a handful of others smuggled out later, all the dogs in the western hemisphere are descended.

The breed is hardy, active, filled with determination, and usually quite long-lived. The Pekingese is a very independent dog with an exasperating stubbornness and an endearing dignity all of its own. Being sturdily built with heavily boned legs, they are surprisingly weighty dogs for their size, weighing up to 12 lb (5·5 kg). The prominent round eye is prone to injury and needs care. The coat is rather coarse and needs a

Toy Dogs

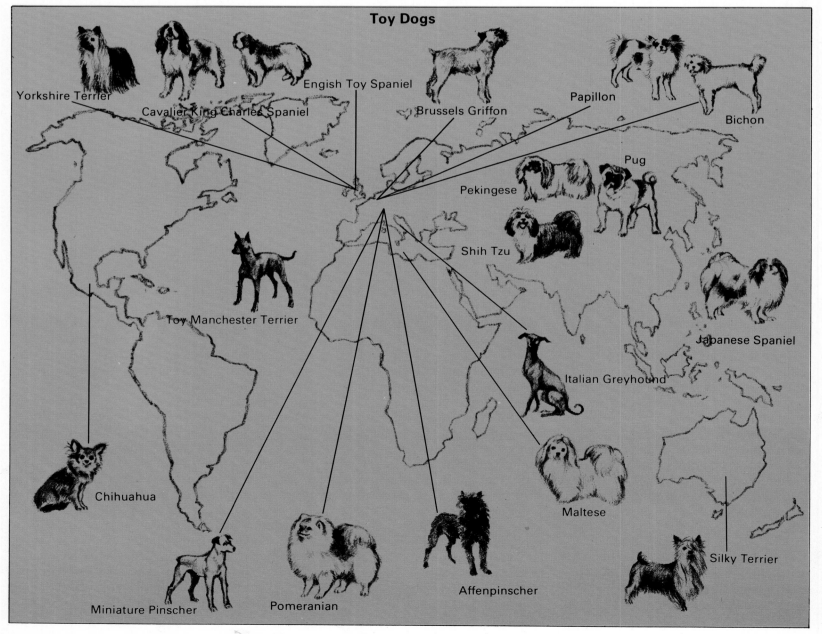

Yorkshire Terrier
Cavalier King Charles Spaniel
Engish Toy Spaniel
Brussels Griffon
Papillon
Bichon
Pekingese
Pug
Shih Tzu
Japanese Spaniel
Toy Manchester Terrier
Italian Greyhound
Chihuahua
Maltese
Silky Terrier
Miniature Pinscher
Pomeranian
Affenpinscher

good deal of brushing. In common with a number of toy breeds the feet of a Pekingese may become very overgrown with hair. In some cases this will mat, making it uncomfortable for the dog to walk, and in all cases it is better trimmed away. Use blunt ended scissors and snip the hair between the pads as well as neatening round the edge of the foot.

The Chihuahua
Another very popular toy breed is the Chihuahua. On average this is the smallest breed of dog in the world and comes from Mexico where it is believed to have descended from the Aztec Sacred Dog, animals which were fattened on rice to form a sacrificial dish for the high priests. The exact connection between these 14th century edible lap-dogs and the 20th century Chihuahua is a little difficult to trace. The only thing that can be said with some certainty is that the Chihuahua really is an all-American breed.

Below: Toy Poodles are a development of this century and have to be under ten inches (255 mm) at the shoulder. In all other respects they should resemble the two larger sizes of Poodle, the Standard and the Miniature. *Below right:* In contrast to the poodles' wealth of coat, the Chinese Crested Dog is entirely bald except for a plume of hair on the tail and a crest of hair on the skull. The skin can be spotted or plain.

They are alert little dogs with saucy expressions and an assured manner. The coat can be any colour and the usual weight is 4–6 lb (1·8–2·7 kg). Unfortunately the smaller the dog the more valuable it is considered to be and some of the very tiny ones, as well as suffering from a skull defect, are too small for their own good health. There are two coat varieties, the smooth with close and glossy hair, and the long-coat which has a soft-textured flat coat with feathering on the legs, a ruff round the neck and a jauntily plumed tail.

Far Eastern toys
The peoples of the Far East were particularly skilled in breeding flat-faced toy dogs. It is probable that the Pug came from China and was introduced into Europe by the Dutch traders of the 16th and 17th centuries who brought it from the East Indies. Again the very flat face means that the Pug can suffer breathing difficulties, particularly in hot weather. The dog is very compact, square and cobby in shape and the fine, short coat needs little except a polish. Though they will probably never be as popular as they were in 18th century England, where every fashionable lady had to have one, the admirers of the Pug are still a numerous and devoted band.

The Shih Tzu from Tibet is another small, snub-nosed, heavily-coated dog which has recently become much better known in the West. Like all the Tibetan

breeds the plumed tail is carried up over the back. The face with its beard, whiskers and topknot gives the dog an expression both arrogant and impudent.

The Japanese Spaniel is a lively, stylish dog. The expression of the large, velvety eyes is demure, which belies the perky nature and fun-loving disposition of these dogs. The parti-coloured coat is long and silky, either black and white or red and white.

European toys
The European toy spaniels are equally distinctive and perhaps better known than the Japanese. The Papillon is the French version, a dog which always seems in the past to have been a court favourite. These little spaniels appear frequently in their owner's portraits. The 16th century dogs were mainly drop-eared but a little later we begin to see a type of dog with an erect ear set obliquely on the head and heavily fringed so as to resemble the butterfly from which the breed takes its name. Papillons are hardy, active dogs with an elegant silky coat, which can be almost any colour. They are among the most easily taught of toy dogs and a number of them have competed in obedience competitions.

The English Toy Spaniel and the Cavalier King Charles Spaniel are both British in origin. The English Toy Spaniel has a very snub nose while the Cavalier has a longer muzzle. Both are natural

versions of bigger relatives. Such is the Pomeranian, a miniscule Spitz type, the smallest of four such breeds recognized in Germany. The toy Pomeranian was produced by British breeders in the late 19th century who succeeded in reducing the size of their German imports very markedly. The result today is a small vivacious ball of fluff, a buoyant little dog often with a great deal to say for itself.

Miniature Greyhounds

Greyhounds were one of the earliest types of dog to be bred with care. Almost as long ago their little cousins, the Italian Greyhounds, were favoured pets of the aristocracy. We do not know how the 70 lb (32 kg) greyhound was scaled down to a miniature weighing 7 lb (3 kg) or less – it all happened so far in the past. The satin coat, the elegance and the air of fragility combine to make this one of the most graceful of small

Left: English Toy Spaniels like these have been court favourites in Europe for many centuries. *Below:* The little Papillon or Butterfly dog is also a very old breed. From the 16th century onwards they have appeared in paintings by such artists as Rubens, Van Dyck, Watteau and Rembrandt. Papillons are very high-spirited and active little dogs.

dogs, needing no special trimming, and both have the characteristic sweet disposition of most of the spaniel tribe. They also retain a lot of the sporting instinct of their larger relatives.

The appeal of the sturdy little Affenpinscher is that of a bewhiskered ragamuffin, a small black urchin carrying himself with comical seriousness. The German name means 'monkey terrier', a very appropriate description for a dog with beetling brows, a prominent bearded chin and a pair of black sparkling eyes alight with devotion and intelligence. The harsh, wiry coat needs very little attention, unlike the Affenpinscher's better known relative the Brussels Griffon. The smartness of this breed owes much to a coat that needs a great deal of stripping and trimming.

Small dogs with flowing white coats, sometimes clipped into curious patterns, have been known for many centuries. The current breeds are the Maltese and the Bichon Frise. The Maltese is the smaller of the two with a coat like spun white sugar, a happy temperament and an active disposition. The Bichon is rather larger with a coat of loose white curls which is trimmed so that the dog looks like a stuffed soft toy.

Many toy breeds are scaled down

popular sport so these are dogs that can give their owners quite a lot of fun in more than one field.

Scaled-down models

Poodles come in three sizes of which the Toy is the smallest and most recent. The Toy Poodle must be 10 in (25·5 cm) or less at shoulder height, but should otherwise resemble the larger Miniature and Standard varieties including having their vivacious, fun-loving temperament. Don't choose a poodle unless you have time for daily grooming and the money for the dog to be clipped every two months or so by a professional.

The Dachshunds, also from the hound group, are a group of breeds small enough to fit into modern living spaces but also sporting enough to please those owners who like their dogs to show a proper interest in the exciting smells of the countryside. There are three different coat types – the glamorous long, the glistening smooth, and the whiskered wire. Each coat variety comes in two different sizes, the Standard and the Miniature.

Another breed in different sizes is the Schnauzer, where you can have either the Giant, Standard or Miniature. The last is by far the most popular, being

Above: Yorkshire Terriers make very sensible pets having all the terrier's love of fun and games. The coat can be shortened to make it less troublesome. The trimmed topknot shown here gives the dog a pert and saucy expression.
Right above: The all-white Maltese is a very glamorous toy dog with the high spirits and energy that seem to go with small stature. *Right below:* Toy Pomeranians are the smallest members of the Spitz group. They make excellent little watch dogs and vivacious companions. The coat should be long, straight and harsh.

dogs. However, it is not as delicate as it might appear though all breeds with coats as thin as this one need a watchful eye kept on them to make sure that they do not become chilled.

Intermediate in size between the Greyhound and the Italian Greyhound is the Whippet. This is a very sporting dog, a hound rather than a toy and the sprinter of the dog world with the fastest acceleration over a short distance of any breed. Strangely, the Whippet is fairly modern. It was produced by the miners of the north of England as a racing and coursing dog towards the end of the last century. Whippet racing is still quite a

about 13 in (33 cm) at the shoulder. This is a hardy, compact and active dog, less aggressive than the larger sizes, but a good guard and watchdog, well able to take care of itself. The coat is harsh and the body hair and head are extensively trimmed. The German word 'schnauzbart' means moustache, and trimming accentuates the dog's beard, eyebrows and whiskers. The usual colour is called pepper and salt, that is a mixture of shades of grey.

Among the smaller working dogs are the short-legged Welsh Corgi and the diminutive Shetland Sheepdog. The latter comes from the Shetland Islands to the north of Scotland. The little Sheltie is a miniature Rough Collie in appearance, intelligence and agility. Sweetness of character and willingness to please are characteristics of the Sheltie as well as of its larger relative.

One of the more popular of the toy dogs is the Silky Terrier, also known as the Sydney Silky after the Australian

Above: The wrinkled face of the Pug has its own quaint charm and so have the snorts and snuffles with which they greet their friends. These are the cobby heavy-weights of the toy dog world. *Left:* As puppies Pekingese are particularly charming, having an air of self importance which seems ridiculous in dogs so small. The density of the fluffy puppy coat shows that these dogs will have a really profuse covering of hair when they are adult. *Right:* The cheeky face and jaunty manner of the West Highland White Terrier have made it many friends. Dirt brushes out easily from such a coarse white coat.

town where it was first developed. Obviously the Yorkshire Terrier is one of the ancestors of the Silky. However, the Silky's coat is only 5–6 in (125–150 mm) long and is flat like fine, glossy silk. The dog is blue with tan markings and should weigh about 8–10 lb (3·5–4·5 kg). Anything smaller is considered a fault and liable to detract from the true terrier characteristics.

The Miniature Pinscher can be considered as a small terrier, since that is what the German word 'pinscher' means. The dog has all the vivacity and gameness of the terrier tribe and a neat and stylish appearance. The glossy smooth coat is either red or black and tan. This is quite an old and well recognized German breed, developed originally as a small ratting dog. Though still an animal of fiery courage, today it is too small for vermin killing. The view that it is simply a small version of the Doberman Pinscher is not correct.

Chapter five
Large Dogs

The giants of the dog world are nearly always dignified and good natured. But they need to be trained from an early age – an unruly dog the size of a St Bernard for example, could wreak havoc in the home.

The really giant breeds of the dog world need a certain amount of special care. Such dogs are slow maturing and do not reach their maximum weight and size until two years of age or more. During this time their diet has to be lavish if they are to achieve the impressive stature that is one of their chief attractions. If we compare small dogs with large, it becomes even clearer how much more food is needed for the heavyweights. A puppy of a toy breed may weight 4 oz (13 g) at birth and grow up to be a 6 lb (2·7 kg) adult. To do this it has to increase its body weight by 24 times. A puppy of a much larger breed may weigh 2 lb (0·9 kg) at birth and weigh over 100 lb (45 kg) as an adult. In other words it is increasing its birth weight over 50 times, so even proportionally it has a lot more growing to do.

If food has to be lavish to keep up the growth rate, exercise has to be carefully graduated, as too much too early again means that growth will be adversely affected. Training, however, should start early since it is imperative that a really large dog has good manners. It is better to start before the dog gets to a size where handling it becomes difficult. Luckily most of the giant breeds are placid and dignified animals when adult, though as youngsters they are liable to have their high-spirited and playful moments.

Large dogs need a good deal of living space. A wagging tail the size of a Great Dane's can do a great deal of damage in a small city apartment for instance. The very heavy breeds not only need space to stretch out but also something soft to lie on, such as a sprung mattress or their own sofa. This is because the dog's weight, pressing on a hard surface, tends

The Great Pyrenees has the dignity which comes with size. The minimum weight for a male is 100 lb (45 kg) and most weigh far more than this. The white coat is a distinctive feature.

to produce calloused and unsightly bald areas of skin on the pressure points such as the elbows.

Though they make impressive guards, some of the really massive breeds are not always the most alert of dogs. Some people advocate keeping a small watchdog to wake up the giant guard dog! None of the very large breeds are long-lived and most are doing very well if they reach nine years.

The St Bernard
One of the most popular of the giants is the St Bernard, a dog which had an almost legendary reputation for rescuing snowbound travellers. Since the Victorians were very fond of sentimentalizing animals and crediting them with the noblest and most unselfish of motives, both the St Bernard and the Newfoundland became canine heroes featuring in many stories and pictures. The monks of the Hospice of Great St Bernard, a monastery perched 2,000 ft (600 m) up on a snowbound Alpine pass, used large dogs to help them in their work of guiding and caring for travellers. The dogs, familiar with the mountain paths guided both monks and lost travellers when all landmarks were obliterated by blizzards and drifts of snow. They were also used as pack animals, bringing supplies up from the valleys. The modern breed is probably heavier and less active than its working ancestor. The broad and massive head has an expression of benevolence and dignity.

The Great Dane
In contrast to the working St Bernard, the Great Dane used to be a hunting dog and the old name of German Boarhound is probably a more descriptive title than its present one. The wild boar is one of the fiercest of quarry, a heavyweight, bad-tempered animal equipped with slashing, ripping rusks. Boarhounds had to be correspondingly

The Irish Wolfhound was bred as a dog of power and speed. The long, punishing jaws enabled the dog to grip and pull down large prey or break the back of smaller game.

powerful and courageous and the Great Dane today is one of the most active as well as one of the tallest of the big breeds. This is a dog that combines elegance and power. The minimum height for a male is 30 in (76 cm) at the shoulder and they are preferred as big as possible provided that they have the weight and power to match. The coat is short and dense, the commonest colours being fawn and brindle.

The Newfoundland
The Newfoundland is also a dog associated with a number of life-saving exploits. This is a breed almost as much at home in water as on land. They are very powerful swimmers and the rather coarse, dense, oily coat is a complete protection against the wet and cold. They were once the fisherman's dog of Newfoundland, used for hauling carts loaded with fish or winter fuel, and for hauling in nets laden with cod. They were expected to retrieve fishing gear lost overboard and to act as courier from boat to shore. The dogs almost seem to have an instinct to go to the aid of anyone in trouble in the water and a number of people have been towed to safety by these powerful swimmers. There are also a number of instances of Newfoundlands taking ropes from shore to boat enabling people to be rescued from ships wrecked on rocky coasts. This is one of the heavyweight breeds, dignified and devoted to its owners, but a dog that has to be led rather than forced.

The Pyrenean Mountain Dog
Whereas the Newfoundland is black (or more rarely white with black patches) the Pyrenean Mountain Dog, or Great

Tallest, smallest
Selective breeding has produced an incredible variety of breeds in the domestic dog. All are believed however to have had the same ancestor.

Irish Wolfhound
The average male must be 32-44 in (81-86 cm) at the shoulder which makes this the tallest breed.

Chihuahua
The smaller the better and animals under 2 lb (450 g) are not uncommon.

St Bernard
The really heavyweight male can weigh more than 200 lb (90 kg).

Greyhound
These dogs exceed 35 mph (56 km/ph).

Above: Underneath the silken curtain of its coat the Afghan Hound is a dog built for speed and has no equal in coursing over a rough and boulder-strewn terrain. The broad, padded feet, the low set hocks and the wide hip bones all enable the dog to twist and turn without slackening pace. *Right:* The Rottweiler from Germany is a handsome heavyweight with a glossy coat.

Pyrenees, as it is called in America, is a snow-white animal. As the name suggests this dog comes from the Pyrenean mountains, a snow-covered range that separates France from Spain. In the lonely mountain pastures this dog was the shepherd's companion and the guardian of the flocks. It was not a dog expected to herd but one that could be relied upon to defend its master's sheep against the marauding wolf or the robber band. The dogs often wore heavily spiked iron collars as a protection. Their efficiency as guards led to them being used as sentries for the chateaux, the great houses of the nobility. By the 17th century they had found favour with the French court and became a companion

Dogs need careful training where other people's livestock are concerned but many surprising animal friendships occur between different species. This Great Dane gently nuzzles two lambs.

of the nobility as well as peasant shepherds. The white coat is thick and heavy enough to withstand the severest of weather. Faint markings of grey or tan are acceptable provided they do not detract from the general impression of majestic white beauty.

The Old English Mastiff
Another heavyweight, and one of the oldest of the giant breeds is the Old English Mastiff, a short-haired giant of a dog with a heavy head and a broad

muzzle. Mastiffs are an ancient type of dog which are represented today by a number of modern breeds such as the Dogue de Bordeaux, the Neopolitan Mastiff and the Old English Mastiff. The latter was found in Britain by the invading Romans in 55 BC. There are accounts of them fighting beside their masters in a vain effort to expel the invaders. The Romans were so impressed that they appointed a special official to collect and send back British Mastiffs to Rome. There they fought in the wild beast and gladiatorial shows arranged by the Emperors to amuse both themselves and the Roman crowd. For much of its history, the Mastiff has been popularly regarded as a fighting dog and a ferocious guard.

Their appearance probably varied a great deal but their courage was unquestioned, and this they share with the modern dog. Today's Mastiff is a quiet, ponderous animal, both dignified and good-natured. The larger it is the better, provided the dog is both massive and sound.

Wolfhounds and Deerhounds
Three other very large breeds belong to the hound group or, more specifically, the gaze-hounds (those that hunt by sight). The tallest and heaviest of these is the Irish Wolfhound. This dog too was known to the Romans and figured largely in Celtic myth and Irish legend. Wolfhounds were the companions of chieftains, courageous and swift to

The Scottish Deerhound needs a spacious country background to look its best. A gentle and graceful dog in repose, the Deerhound's dignity has won it many admirers.

overtake their quarry. They went into battle beside their masters and were big and strong enough to pull enemies from their horses. Such dogs were sent as princely gifts from one king to another so that their fame spread far beyond Ireland. With the extinction of the wolf in Ireland in the early 18th century, the breed also very nearly slipped into oblivion. It was only saved from complete extinction by a 19th century sportsman who devoted 20 years of his life to reviving both the dog and people's interest in it. Today the Irish Wolfhound is rarely used in the sporting field but the size and strength of the dog are undiminished.

The Russian Wolfhound or Borzoi was also used for coursing wolves. Wolf coursing in pre-revolutionary Russia was a sport enjoyed by the wealthy and conducted with a certain amount of ceremony. Usually two Borzois were slipped after a wolf. They were expected to overtake it and pin it down until the huntsman arrived. The Russian Czar presented some of these dogs to British royalty. It became fashionable to own these extremely elegant dogs with their high-stepping springy stride and silky coats. Not only did they adorn stately homes, they added glamour to film stars and models. Luckily the breed survived this sort of publicity. They are not dogs for small homes as they need plenty of space to be seen at their best, but they are never likely to lack admirers.

The Scottish Deerhound is another dog built for speed. Coursing the deer in Scotland is a sport that was superseded by deer stalking with a high-powered rifle. Enough people, however, appreciated the dog's gentle and dignified nature, and its abilities as a poaching dog, to keep the breed in existence. Once dog showing became an accepted sport, the Deerhound attracted its own band of admirers – a staunch and discriminating band who value the dog's grace and good nature. Unlike many breeds the Deerhound appears to have changed scarcely at all over the centuries and in this sense may be described as a piece of living history.

Other large dogs
Most of the dog giants measure 30 in (76 cm) or more at the shoulder. While not quite making the height and weights of the breeds already mentioned, there are plenty of other pretty hefty dogs.

Two Spitz breeds from widely separated areas – the bear-hunting Akita from Japan and the Alaskan Malamute – pack a lot of weight into their very sturdy frames. The Rottweiler from Germany is another powerful dog. This breed was a cattle dealer's dog, one that both drove the beasts and guarded the takings. Again it almost disappeared when road transport took over, but got a second lease of life as a police and army dog.

Another very robust hound is the Norwegian Elkhound, a big, grey spitz-type animal. It is reputed to have accompanied the Vikings on their marauding raids throughout Europe. The thick coat is abundant, coarse and weather-resistant, as befits a dog of the north, bred for hunting the big game of those latitudes, the bear and the elk. In its native land this breed is still used to hunt the elk. It is expected to track and then hold at bay its adversary until the hunter arrives. The short-coupled muscular frame of the Elkhound enables it to dodge and twist with great dexterity, avoiding the elk's antlers.

The Rhodesian Ridgeback is another hunting dog of power and substance. South Africa saw the development of this breed where Boer farmers needed a dog that would hunt any sort of game, guard the farm and be tough enough to stand the rigours of life in the bush. About 100 years ago Ridgebacks were introduced into Rhodesia where they were used to hunt lion. The dog's short, dense coat is red or wheaten and the distinctive feature from which they get their name is the hair along the spine which grows the opposite way to the rest of the coat, creating a ridge.

The Great Pyrenees was a guard dog for the flocks and herds which grazed the high mountain slopes dividing France and Spain. As such it had to be large enough to tackle wolves.

Chapter six
Choosing a Puppy

What is the best way of choosing a dog to suit you? How do you find the right puppy? All puppies are appealing, but first you must consider how much time, money and care you can afford to give it. It is not fair to keep a dog and then leave it alone all day, or buy a sporting dog and never give it a chance to use its instincts.

Dogs come in many sizes and shapes with different temperaments and personalities. How do you find out which dog will suit you? The problem deserves a lot of thought. When you take a puppy into your family you are taking on an animal for whose physical and mental needs you will be responsible for the next ten years or more. The first thing to consider is not what will suit you but whether your way of life is such that you can really afford to keep a dog: not only afford the money but afford the time and afford the care. Dogs are adaptable, which is why they have been so successful in their partnership with man. However, they do have basic needs and these are the owner's responsibility.

The social instinct
Dogs are basically pack animals, not solitary ones. They need companionship and are only too happy if it is their master's. Possibly the happiest dogs are those who share their owner's lives daily. This is not often possible but the other extreme, where the dog is shut up alone for nine to ten hours while all the family goes out to work is a form of unimaginative cruelty. If there is no one about during the day, you may need a burglar alarm but you don't need a dog. Of course dogs have to be left alone sometimes and you need to accustom your dog to staying quietly, but these periods of solitude should be the exception, not a way of life.

How much does it cost?
The actual expense of buying a dog is little enough compared with the cost of its keep over the years. The quantity that dogs eat can vary very greatly with the amount of work and exercise that they

Toy Spaniels like these Cavalier King Charles have affectionate and biddable natures. The chestnut-and-white colouring shown here is called Blenheim.

get. The following rough guide will help you calculate the size of animal you can afford to keep. A toy breed may eat up to 10 oz (280 g) daily, a breed about the size of a German Shepherd 2 lb (0·9 kg) daily, and a giant breed from 4 lb (1·8 kg) upwards.

There are, of course, other expenses as well. Your dog may become ill or have an accident. All dogs need preventative inoculations. Both mean that there will be veterinary fees to pay. Many people take their dogs on holiday with them but you may want to board your dog in kennels instead. This will mean having the forethought to book well in advance if you are going away in a peak period, and more fees to pay.

Other things depend on how much time you have available for your pet. All dogs need exercise and this means someone has to take them out. Turning a dog loose in a securely fenced plot will not exercise it. Nor should any dog be allowed out on its own. If not picked up as a stray, such animals cause a great deal of mischief. If you are not with your dog when it is out you cannot be sure that is is not the cause of a traffic accident, or know that it is not worrying someone's livestock. What you can be

Top: A Sealyham puppy like this is a great comic. Though tough little terriers, with plenty of courage, Sealyhams manage to combine this with the roly-poly charm of a born comic. *Above:* The Dalmatian is one of the most easily recognized breeds, and a dog with a dozen nicknames. They were originally stable dogs, keeping down the rats and accompanying the horses.

sure of is that it will be eating someone's garbage and fouling where it should not. Most pet dogs could do with more exercise than they get. A daily walk of 3–4 miles (4–6 km), part of it off the lead, should be a must for all except some toy dogs. What is more it is good for their owners as well. The larger and more racily built a dog is, the more exercise it needs. Provided they are adequately fed and worked up to the exercise gradually, few healthy dogs can have too much walking.

Grooming also takes time. Daily grooming is better for the dog's health but with a smooth-coated breed you can settle, if you wish, for a regular weekly session of half an hour or so. However, if you choose a long-coated breed, a daily grooming period is a must. Some breeds also need trimming or clipping at regular intervals. The dog can go to a beauty parlour or you can learn to do this kind of barbering yourself. It does, however, take a lot of patient practice and, in the case of clipping, some rather expensive equipment.

Purebred or mongrel?

Whether to buy a purebred (pedigree) dog or a mongrel is another consideration. The purebred will cost more but in relation to the cost of the dog's keep over a lifetime, it is a small enough price to pay for pride of ownership. There is no evidence to support the view that mongrels are either healthier or more intelligent than purebred animals. Just as in humans, intelligence in dogs is a very variable commodity. If mongrels had a monopoly of brains and health, they would be used by those businesses that rely on trained dogs. However, all such organizations use purebreds. One of the reasons is that they know exactly what they are getting in the way of size and looks, as well as a fair idea of the kind of temperament.

All the ills that dogs can get are pretty evenly distributed throughout the canine race. The only point to be watched is that any breed that has a particularly exaggerated shape may have a health weakness. Examples would include very long backs, very flattened muzzles, protruding or very small eyes.

Dog or bitch?

The question of whether to buy a dog or a bitch will also arise and this is very much a matter of personal preference. There is quite a marked difference between the sexes in some breeds with the males being larger and more outward looking. They may also be more aggressive and inclined to roam. However, loyalty, affection, guarding ability and obedience are qualities found in the individual dog rather than in a particular sex.

Bitches come 'into season' or 'on heat' twice a year. This is a period of up to three weeks when they are sexually attractive to male dogs and have to be kept closely confined if you do not want them to have a litter. There are now various ways of postponing or suppressing a bitch's season so this does not have to be drawback.

Most people choose to buy a puppy. The advantages are that the dog will grow up as part of the family and its behaviour will be moulded to suit your particular way of life. Do not, however, reject an adult dog out of hand. Many have to be found new homes through no fault of their own. Families separating,

housing difficulties or an owner's death may all be reasons for a dog needing rehousing. Do not feel that an adult dog will not become attached to you. The loyalty and affection that such a dog will show you depends far more upon your treatment than the dog's age. Many animal sanctuaries have adult dogs to rehouse. Get any animal obtained this way checked by a vet and also try to have the animal on a week's trial. In this way you can find out if the dog has any bad habits that you cannot stand.

Choosing a breed

If you have decided you would like a purebred dog, the choice of breeds does seem a little bewildering. Deciding what you can afford to feed, house and exercise may cut out a number of breeds

Above: The Golden Retriever is one of the kindliest and most adaptable of the retrieving breeds. Puppies of any breed are born short-coated, and these will develop the soft feathering of their mother as they grow older. *Right:* Cocker Spaniels have been top favourites on both sides of the Atlantic for many years, perhaps because of their ever-wagging tails.

automatically. Try to look very critically at those which are left and which appeal to you. Read about the breeds. Their history will tell you something about the temperament and behaviour to expect.

Many terriers were bred to show reckless courage in the face of danger. They had to locate their enemies, often below ground, and bark and bite when

One month old – two milk meals, two meat meals per day.

Three months old – one milk meal, two meat meals.

Feeding a dog
Dogs are adaptable and can thrive on a wide range of diets. But carnivorous animals, like the dog, need meat or a similar protein as the main ingredient in their diet.

Six months old – two meat meals, plus some biscuits.

Adult dog – one main meat meal, plus biscuits, bone, etc.

Puppy care

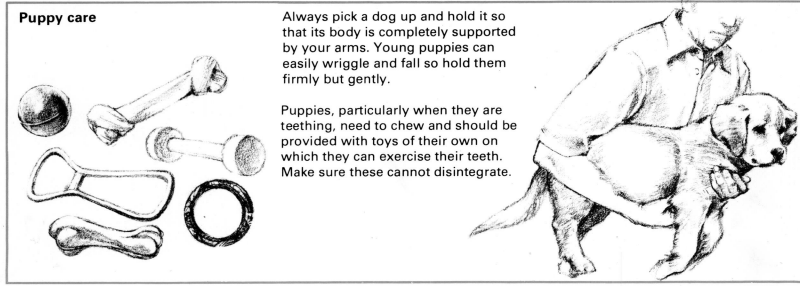

Always pick a dog up and hold it so that its body is completely supported by your arms. Young puppies can easily wriggle and fall so hold them firmly but gently.

Puppies, particularly when they are teething, need to chew and should be provided with toys of their own on which they can exercise their teeth. Make sure these cannot disintegrate.

they found them. Many of this group, therefore, tend to be noisy, excitable, aggressive and fond of digging!

If the breed that appeals to you has been kept for many generations as a watchdog, then you would expect it to be aloof, if not downright suspicious, of strangers, and alert to anything unusual. Many of the hound breeds, raised to use their noses, are conveniently deaf to all commands and inclined to roam when following that all-enticing scent. A lot of the sheepdog and gundog breeds are happier dogs if they are given something to do. It does not really matter what form the training takes. Bored and closely confined dogs all too often become destructive, noisy and neurotic.

Try to make sure that you see some adults of the breed you finally choose, before you commit yourself to a puppy. One of the best places to do this, of course, is at a dog show. Not only will you be able to see all shapes and sizes, if you watch carefully, you will also be able to pick out the breeds which tend to be noisy and aggressive from the more placid and good-natured.

Finding your puppy

By far the best person to buy a puppy from is its breeder. Puppies in pet shops and dealer's kennels have already suffered the stress of a change of environment and a change of diet. They may already have travelled a long way in far from ideal conditions, and they may well have met some infection.

To find a dog breeder of the breed you want may take a little time and trouble. Again, a dog show may provide you with a chance to talk to several breeders and, if they do not have any puppies themselves, they may very well know of people who do. Magazines about dogs usually carry breeder's advertisements and, perhaps more useful still, the names and addresses of the breed club secretaries. Each variety of dog has one or more breed clubs looking after its interests and these are sources of information both about the breeds and the owners of kennels.

Always make haste slowly when buying a dog. If you have the opportunity, go and see several litters and remember always that what you need above all is a healthy, good-tempered animal. The best age to buy is when the puppy is about eight weeks old. At this age temperament is difficult to assess but the very nervous and withdrawn puppy will show up. The surroundings of the litter should be clean and spacious and the puppies themselves clear-eyed with loose, supple skin and a well-rounded appearance.

Opposite: A white Miniature Poodle bitch feeds her almost-weaned puppies. She knows that they are past the stage of depending on her for food and will move off smartly when she has had enough of them. *Right:* A Beagle puppy of this age will be filled with curiosity about the world in general and is ready to leave home and become someone's pet. Remember though that babies like this still need plenty of rest and protection from dangers that they do not understand. Such hazards as broken glass, electric wiring or household poisons must be kept out of a puppy's way. *Below:* In every litter the bullies and the greedy ones will take more than their fair share if all are fed together as shown here. Puppies should have their own dishes and with long-eared breeds like these Basset hounds, deep narrow dishes will keep the ears out of the food.

Before you view a litter make a list of the questions you want to ask. It is only too easy to forget them in the excitement of watching pups at play. Most dog breeders are only too anxious that their animals go to the right sort of home and will be very willing to discuss anything you feel you need to know. Indeed you may find you are questioned closely about your suitability as a dog owner. A dedicated dog breeder will care very much about where his puppies go and will try to make sure that you are the right sort of person to own his particular breed. This may help to save you from making an expensive mistake and is the kind of service you will not find at the pet supermarket.

If you want to reserve a puppy in a litter that is not yet old enough to leave you may be asked to leave a deposit of part of the purchase price. This deposit is non-returnable should you fail to return and complete the purchase. There is a generally recognized best age for selling pups, and puppies booked and then not collected involve their breeder in extra trouble and expense. It is also as well to remember that you are unlikely to recoup the purchase price of your puppy should you, for any reason, want to sell it at a later date. Very few people want halfgrown or adolescent dogs, and tend to view with suspicion an animal that is on the market at this sort of age since it is likely to have faults of some kind.

Chapter seven
Caring for your Dog

Your dog is a faithful companion to you, and reliant on you for its well-being. From puppy-hood it needs the same care that you would expect yourself – balanced and regular meals, play and exercise, comfort and care when ill.

A puppy bought at eight weeks old or so is still a baby needing warmth, affection, plenty of rest and small frequent meals. With your new purchase you should have received a pedigree and the papers registering the dog with the Kennel Club.

Feeding a puppy
You should also ask for a diet sheet listing exactly what the puppy has been used to eating up to now. It is an advantage if you can keep to exactly the same diet for the first day or two. The puppy then has a chance to settle down in its new surroundings before having to cope with unfamiliar food. You may wish to change the diet completely but it must be done very gradually. Sudden changeovers, even with adult dogs, can cause digestive upsets which a more cautious introduction of the different food can avoid.

An eight week old puppy should have four meals a day and these are usually two milk and cereal-based meals, and two meat meals. Remove the dish as soon as the dog starts to lose interest but make sure that fresh water is always available. Animals should always be fed from their own dishes, never from yours. It is worthwhile buying something that combines the virtues of easy cleaning with a shape that is difficult for a dog to tip over.

By the time the dog is three months old, the meals can be cut in number to three, and at six months to two. Obviously the amount of each feed is increased. From six months or so until they are mature, most dogs actually need more food than they will as adults. This is because not only are they still growing, they are also full of adolescent energy and high spirits. Some people

This young owner is starting the right way by teaching her St Bernard puppy to enjoy a daily comb. Grooming accustoms the dog to being handled and should be a joy for owner and pet.

like to keep their dogs on two meals a day, and certainly the giant breeds need the extra for some considerable time and this can best be supplied by offering morning and evening feeds. Most adult dogs, however, can manage quite well on one meal a day.

Bringing your puppy home
The first few days of your puppy's life with you are very important from the point of view of building up confidence and trust. Hopefully you will have been able to fetch your puppy yourself, so that it did not have the frightening experience of being sent on its own. Many puppies are travel sick so be prepared with tissues, old towels and words of comfort. When you get the puppy home the first thing it will want to do is produce a large puddle so put it down in the right place immediately. Then you can praise your dog as the first step towards house training, and also congratulate yourself on your forethought.

All dogs should have their own bed where they can rest undisturbed. Though it is tempting to buy a lot for a new arrival in the family, a cardboard carton of an appropriate size makes the best puppy bed. If you pick one with a lid as well and merely cut a small entrance hole, you can be sure that your puppy will feel secure and will be better able to keep itself warm. It is of the very greatest importance that anywhere that a dog sleeps is dry and draught free. A cardboard carton at least ensures the latter and can be thrown away as soon as it is outgrown or falls apart.

For the first two or three nights your pup will miss the warmth and comfort of its litter mates. Providing a well wrapped hot water bottle or even a soft toy may do something to minimize the puppy's feeling of loss. All dogs eventually have to get used to being alone for part of the time but you may wish to have the dog's box near you for the first night or two so that you can reassure the frightened and

lonely newcomer.

The feathering on the back of the legs is a favourite place for mats to form. It should, however, be brushed and combed out gently so as not to break off too much hair and spoil the dog's looks.

One of the most useful pieces of equipment for a puppy is a small pen where it can be left with a bed and its toys in safety whenever you cannot directly keep an eye on it. Not all toys manufactured for dogs are safe, any more than all toys made for children, so choose with care. A large raw marrowbone provides the most amusement for dogs of any age. Small bones, and in particularly poultry and fish bones, must not be given. Rawhide toys are very good. They are not easy for a dog to take apart and the pieces are meant to be eaten anyway. Rubber and plastic toys need to be watched. Some stand up to hard wear and puppy teeth. Others disintegrate and must be removed promptly before the pieces get swallowed, possibly causing some internal blockage.

The growth period
Puppies, like children, grow by fits and starts, sometimes appearing very leggy and awkward and then gradually filling out. It is sometimes helpful to feed a vitamin and mineral supplement throughout the growth period. Whether this is needed depends very much on what else you are feeding. If you are feeding a manufactured food that is already fortified in this way, then you could do harm by overdosing. Normally dietary supplements are only needed during growth, pregnancy, lactation (when a bitch is feeding her puppies) and in old age.

By the time they are four to five weeks old, puppies have grown a set of 28 milk teeth, small and needle-sharp. They start to lose these and replace them with a set of 42 permanent teeth when they are

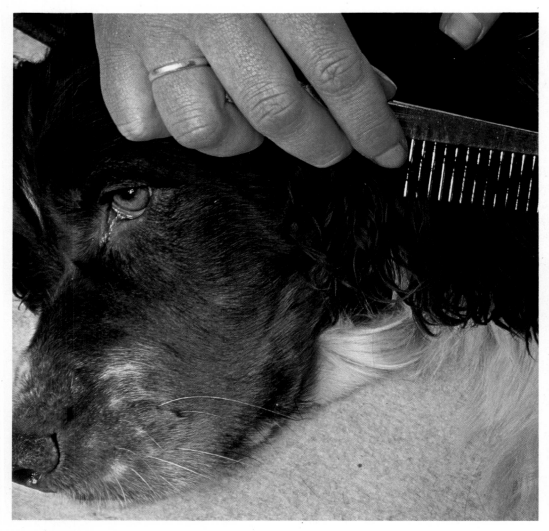

Left: Grooming is very much easier if the right tools are used. The long, silky coat of a Cocker Spaniel needs a medium-bristle brush and a wide-toothed steel comb with blunt teeth. Gentle but regular use keeps the coat untangled. *Below:* Special clippers are needed to cut a dog's claws. Cutting in the wrong place can be intensely painful for a dog so get an expert to show you how to do it. *Right:* A stiff bristle brush is suitable for a wire-coated breed like this Norwich Terrier. Grooming should get through to the skin to stimulate the circulation.

about four to five months. Most puppies have little trouble with teething though all need plenty to chew to help loosen the old teeth. A few puppies become off-colour and feverish. Rubbing their inflamed gums with a soothing lotion may help.

Dog diseases

Two of the most serious diseases that dogs can catch are distemper and viral hepatitis. Distemper is common and, if not fatal, can leave a dog with chronic weaknesses. Puppies are, of course, very susceptible. Viral hepatitis is a liver complaint that is equally debilitating. In the past dogs had little or no protection and all breeders dreaded the infection reaching their kennels and spreading through their stock. The development of vaccines, which will protect dogs not only against distemper and hepatitis but also leptospiral infections, has removed much of the fear and worry that owners used to have.

It is vital that your puppy is inoculated and receives booster shots when advised by your veterinary surgeon. There are various inoculation programmes. In some cases puppies will be protected before they are sold. If so, check exactly what they have been given and when it should be renewed. You should receive

a certificate telling you this. If your puppy has not yet had its shots then you must be very careful to keep it away from all strange dogs and also from places where such dogs have been exercised. Check with your vet which vaccination programme he advises.

Feeding your dog

The dog is a carnivore, that is a meat-eating animal. You can tell this from its teeth which are designed to grip and tear off chunks of flesh, which are then bolted down rather than chewed. Wild dogs hunt and kill for their food but do not confine themselves to eating only the red muscle meat of their victim. They eat the stomach contents, the offal (such as liver and heart) and they crack the big bones to get at the marrow inside. Since the prey of the wild dog will be a herbivorous animal (one that eats grass), the stomach contents will provide the dog with a portion of partially digested vegetation, all of which is necessary for the dog's health.

Obviously the pet dog has its food provided for it. However, you will see from the above that feeding your dog on steak alone would not be a kindness. Indeed it would lead to the animal having various deficiency diseases. The diet you provide should have something

like 60% protein (such as meat), 30% carbohydrate (such as biscuits), with about 10% fat (animal or vegetable). The pet food industry takes feeding your dog very seriously and provides a wide range of foods. They include tins, frozen blocks, semi-moist foods in plastic sachets and complete dried foods in pellet form. The latter provide all the nutrients a dog needs but, as they have had all the moisture removed from them, it is even more important that the dog has free access to lots of fresh water.

Which way you feed your dog is up to you but choose a well known brand name and read the label very carefully so that you can follow the manufacturer's instructions. You will have to adjust the amount you give to your own particular dog's requirements. A very active dog will need far more food to fuel its energy than one that lies around all day. Do not let your dog get fat. It will shorten its life, spoil its fun and be as bad for it as it would be for you. However, you cannot expect the dog to ration itself. You are the one responsible for that. Don't give your dog anything sweet in the form of titbits. Dogs don't need sugar but they can get just as hooked on it as humans can with the same ruinous effect on their teeth and on their waistlines.

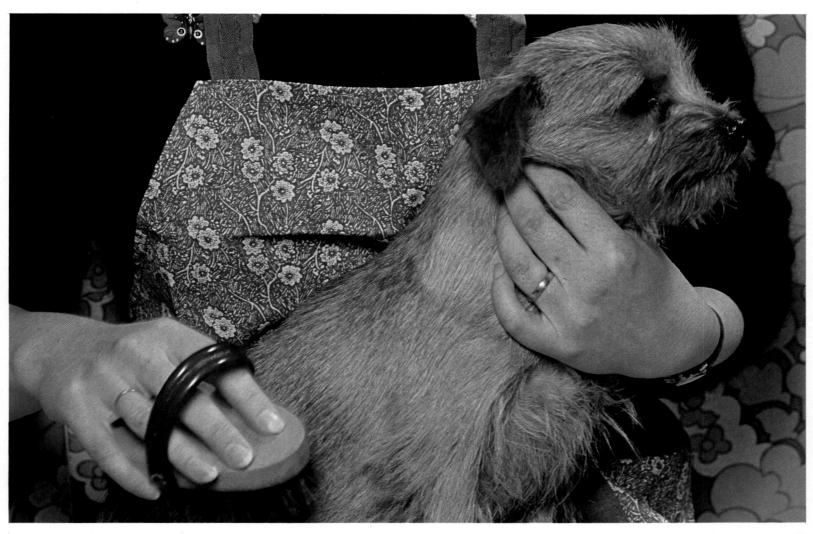

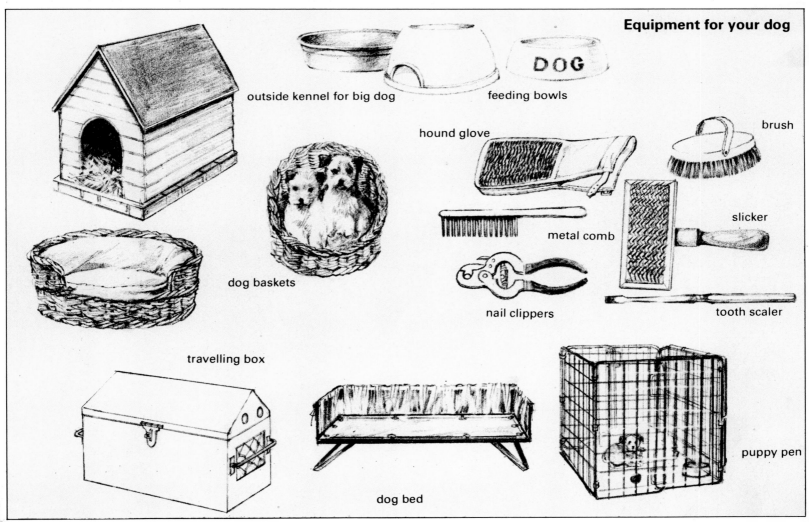

Equipment for your dog

outside kennel for big dog

feeding bowls

DOG

hound glove

brush

dog baskets

metal comb

slicker

nail clippers

tooth scaler

travelling box

dog bed

puppy pen

Equipment

Equipment for an adult dog should be chosen with care with a view to it lasting the dog's lifetime. A lightweight collar and lead that is soon outgrown and a carton for a bed are perfectly adequate for a puppy. Collars for adult dogs should either be made of good quality leather or of nylon. Remember that your dog's life could depend on the strength of the collar and leash. If you choose leather, oil it frequently to keep it supple and strong. Types of collar are much a matter of fashion. Broad, heavily studded collars are chosen by bull terrier

owners. Wide collars of thin suede show off the elegant length of a whippet's neck. A rolled leather collar will mark the neck hair less if your dog is long-coated.

The best tag for attaching your name and address to a collar is an engraved metal one. Plastic does not seem to stand up to the hard wear. The slip collar or check chain is a useful training device which is discussed in the next chapter. Leads need to be strong enough to hold the weight of the dog and the clip at the end should be of the trigger hook type. Do not be tempted to buy a chain because you think it will be stronger.

Chains are only suitable for tethering an animal. They are too uncomfortable to use as a leash and, at the worst, can injure the dog or hurt your hands.

The bed for an adult dog should be easy to clean and either be off the floor or completely enclosed so as to eliminate draughts. It should also be big enough for the dog to lie out flat on its side. Old dogs in particular sometimes find it difficult to curl up and prefer to stretch out. Needless to say the dog's bed should be a place where it can rest undisturbed whenever it wants. A crate is another useful purchase. Your dog can

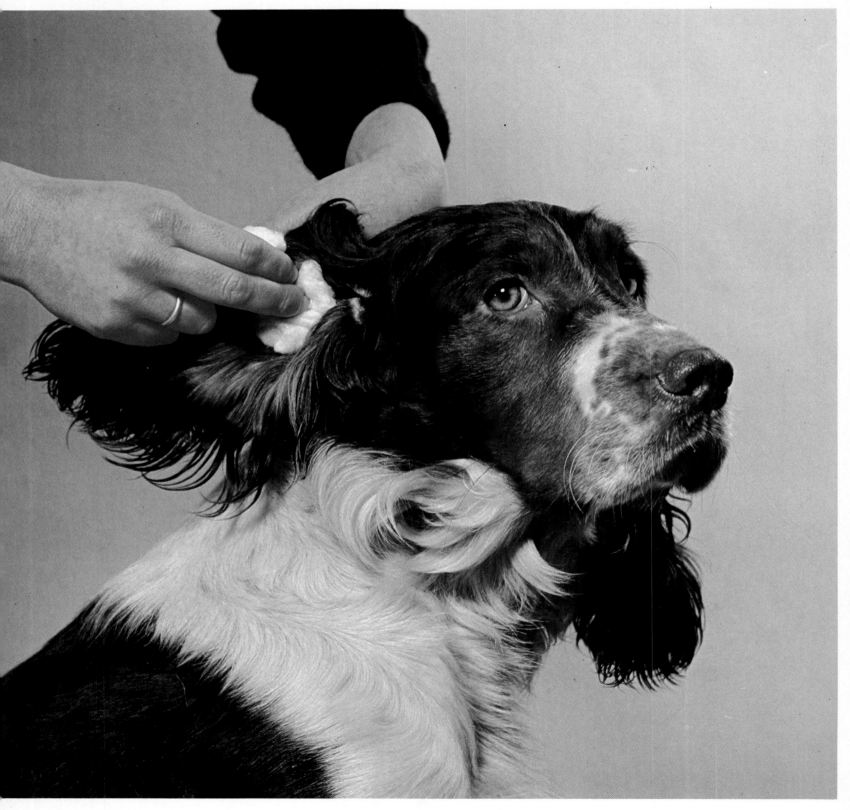

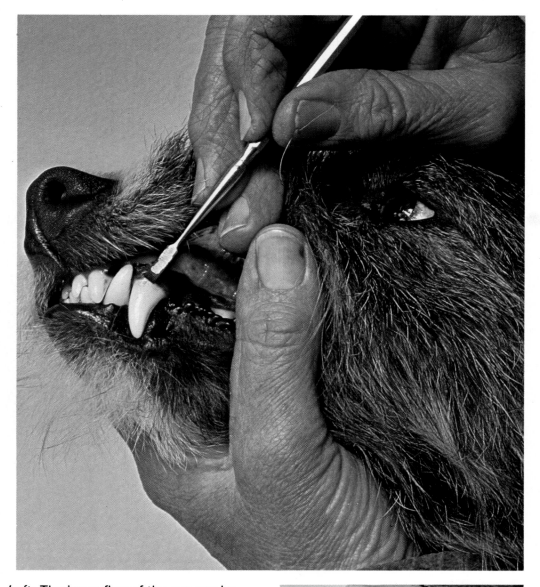

Left: The inner flap of the ear can be cleaned with cottonwool soaked with olive oil or baby oil. Never put anything down the ear canal itself and keep water out of the ears by plugging them with cottonwool when the dog has a bath. *Above:* Tartar can be scraped off the teeth with a dental scraper. If left too long it can cause the gum to recede and the tooth to become loose. *Right:* A dog will open its mouth if pressure is applied to the lips against the teeth. A pill should be pushed to the back of the throat and the mouth then held shut until the dog has swallowed.

travel in it in the car or be left shut up when you go out for short periods. However the convenience of a crate often leads to its abuse with dogs spending long hours shut up unnecessarily. Some show dogs suffer this way with a deterioration in both mental and physical health.

Exercise

If you plan to keep your dog outside you must provide housing that is dry and windproof. Though sunlight is good for dogs, they must also have shade. Dogs

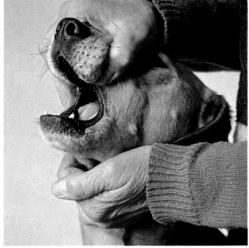

in fenced runs rarely exercise themselves so this still should be a daily chore. In cities where dogs must be leashed you need to choose a small breed that will be satisfied with enough exercise this way. Teaching your dog to chase and bring back a ball provides more exercise. Make sure that the ball is too large to get wedged in the dog's throat. Never be tempted to throw stones for your dog. Dogs have lost eyes and teeth when their owners have done just that. Swimming is also a good form of exercise. Coaxing a

puppy into shallow water is a good way to start. Frightening an animal by throwing it in is an excellent way of putting it off the idea for life. All dogs *can* swim. Some dogs, like some humans, just don't take to the idea.

The bitch in season

If you own a bitch, then she will come into season for the first time usually between six months and a year old, and then at roughly six monthly intervals. The first sign of a season is that the bitch's vulva will become swollen and she will have a blood-stained discharge. Dogs will be attracted to her by the scent but she will not be so interested in them for another ten days or so. At that stage she will be as anxious to meet a dog as they will be to get to her which means that you will have to take the utmost care to keep her shut up.

There are a number of ways of preventing a bitch from coming into season. The most drastic is spaying, a major operation to remove the reproductive organs so that the bitch can never have a litter. This should not be done until the bitch is mature. It is also possible to give a course of pills or an injection to prevent a season and you should discuss this with your vet.

Looking after an old dog

As a dog gets old, and most are showing signs of age by nine or ten years, it should be allowed to take life at its own pace. Sight and hearing may not be as good as they were so make allowances if an old dog seems inattentive. Now it is more important than ever to keep the dog slim, but at the same time the food should be of the highest quality with an extra vitamin supplement. Check that the old dog's bed is warm, dry and comfortable to help ease aching joints.

Grooming

Grooming should be a regular chore. Get the right equipment as this makes a great deal of difference to the dog's comfort. A smooth-coated animal needs a short bristled brush, a hound glove and a polishing duster. Brush with the lie of the coat, being quite firm as this helps to massage the skin. Use your hands to groom the dog as well. With fingers bent pull them through the coat from the tail towards the head. Finally smooth down the coat with the palms of your hands. This kind of grooming removes the dead hair and stimulates the circulation and thus, indirectly, the hair growth. What is more, most dogs love it. A steel comb is necessary with many breeds to remove tangles. Choose one where the teeth have well rounded ends that cannot

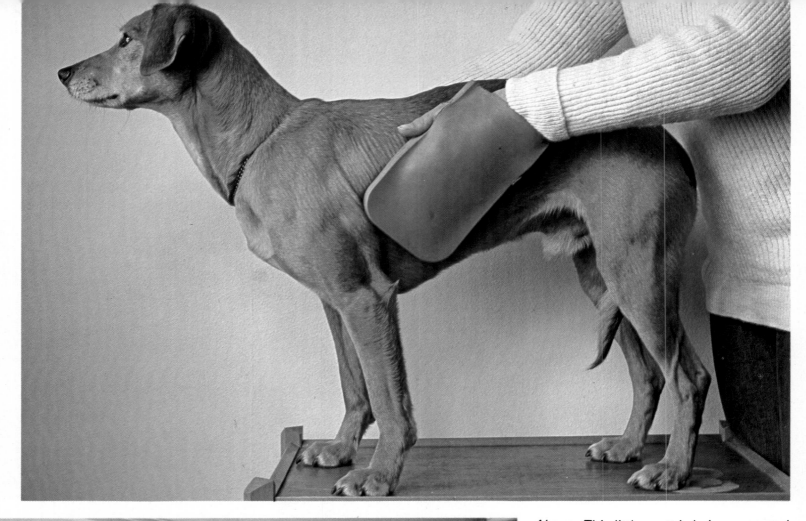

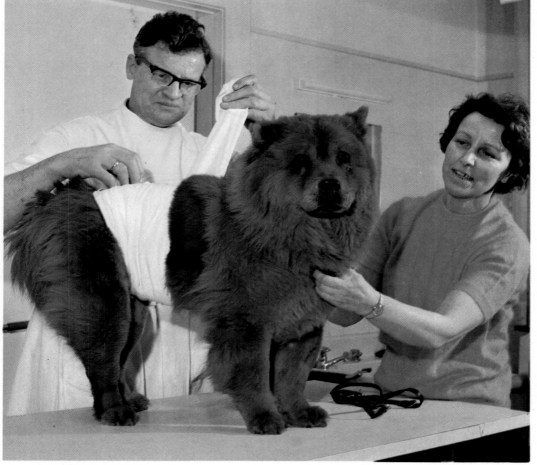

Above: This little mutt is being groomed with a rubber hound glove, the palm of which is covered with rows of small rubber teeth. This is an excellent aid to removing dead coat and dirt from a smooth-coated dog. A rub down with a polishing cloth will complete the session. *Left:* Training your dog to stand still and be handled by strangers can be a great help when your vet needs the patient's co-operation. *Right:* Not all dogs like being dried with a hair drier but it is the most efficient and certainly the quickest method.

Regular grooming should also include care of the ears, eyes, nails and teeth. Clean the inside of the ear-flap with cottonwool moistened with olive oil or baby oil. Never attempt to poke anything down the ear itself. Try to keep the inside of the ear free from hair by jerking it out a few hairs at a time. This should not distress the dog unless you try to remove too many at once or unless the ear is already sore. Signs of ear trouble that need professional attention include the dog shaking or rubbing its head on the ground, an ear which feels hot and tender to the touch, an evil smelling discharge or a lot of brown sticky wax.

Dogs receiving adequate exercise should not need to have their claws cut. You should, however, keep an eye on the dewclaws found on the fifth toe which some dogs have a little way up on the inside of the leg. As they receive little wear, some dewclaws occasionally need

scratch the skin. A stripping knife is the trimming tool used on many wire-coated breeds. To use it successfully you need patience and practice. Try to watch an expert at work first. The best and most thorough grooming for a long-coated breed is done with brushing and yet

more brushing. This must be done in layers so that the brush gets right down to the skin and being systematic makes sure you have covered every inch. The difficult areas where matting is liable to occur are inside the thighs and in the hollows behind the elbows.

clipping. You need special clippers and, in the case of a dog with overgrown nails, get an expert to show you how it should be done. There are nerves and blood vessels growing down inside the nail and if you cut this living quick you will hurt the dog.

Giving the dog plenty to chew helps keep the teeth clean. Tartar (a brown, furry substance) sometimes forms round the base of the canines, the big eye teeth. This should be scraped off with a dental tool.

Grooming will also enable you to check your dog for skin parasites, the commonest of which are fleas. The dog will scratch and you may see a small, red-brown, quickly moving insect. Small black specks on the skin are another indication. The best method of control is a parasiticidal bath which will also kill lice, seen as slow-moving whitish specks. Ticks, which look like greyish peas attached to the skin, need to be dabbed with alcohol and pulled off. The

commonest internal parasites are the roundworm and the tapeworm. Roundworms infest puppies and are passed with the faeces. They look like small pieces of yellow string. Your puppy should have been wormed twice before the age of eight weeks and if the breeder says that this has been done then you should not need to give a further worming pill until the dog is six months. Make sure both the pill and the dosage are correct. Tapeworms are more often found in adult dogs, their flat white segments look like grains of rice. Again a pill from your vet is the answer.

Caring for a sick dog

Your dog's health depends on you so learn to watch your pet carefully. Unusual behaviour may mean something is wrong. One of the best ways to check is to take the dog's temperature. This is taken in the rectum so coat the bulb end of a thermometer with vaseline. Keep the dog standing by putting an arm under its stomach, raise the dog's tail and insert the thermometer for a third of its length into the rectum. Your dog may think this is undignified but it doesn't hurt. Normal temperature

Above left: A dog injured in a road accident should be carried on an improvised stretcher. Remember that a dog in pain is liable to bite. *Left:* Teach your dog to enjoy wading and swimming. The latter is just as good exercise for dogs as it is for humans. *Above right:* An ecstatic roll gets rid of the itches! Unfortunately many dogs seem to like a good roll straight after a bath so watch your dog carefully for a while when he has just been dried. *Below:* A Saluki travelling at speed is one of the most graceful of sights. The whole dog is a streamlined silhouette.

is 101.5°F, and more than a degree above or below this is suspicious.

Do not rely on giving medicines in food as many sick dogs will not eat. Give liquid medicines from a small bottle rather than a spoon. Tilt the dog's head up with its mouth closed and pull out the corner of the lip to make a pocket into which the liquid can be slowly poured. To give pills, seat the dog in a corner so that it cannot back away. Open the mouth and push the pill as far down the throat as possible. Then hold the mouth closed until the dog has swallowed.

Illness needs professional diagnosis and treatment but the actual nursing of a sick dog is often better done at home by a loved and trusted owner than by an impersonal if well-trained veterinary nurse in an animal hospital. The strain of different surroundings and strange smells makes most animals uneasy which is not ideal for a quick recovery. Also a tremendous amount can be done towards a sick dog's recovery by the kind and reassuring attitude of its owner who must remain calm and cheerful however worrying or distressing the situation turns out to be.

Three things are vital to successful nursing and these are warmth, peace and quiet, and cleanliness. The warmth must be constant. When the dog goes outside to relieve itself, it should wear a coat made from a piece of old blanket or similar.

Sick and convalescent dogs often become faddy feeders. If your vet has specified a diet then this must be adhered to, but otherwise food must be nourishing and easily digested. Honey in milky drinks is safe to give in most circumstances, and so are broths made from white meat such as chicken and rabbit. Spoonfuls fed at frequent intervals will keep a dog going until it is strong enough to take an interest. To tempt a dog with no appetite calls for a certain amount of ingenuity. Sometimes strongly smelling foods such as cheese or fish will do the trick.

Chapter eight
Training your Dog

Training must begin from the moment you get your puppy home. The principle is always the same: never scold about something already done. Your puppy will not connect his crime with the punishment. Praise, above all, will teach your dog what it should or should not do.

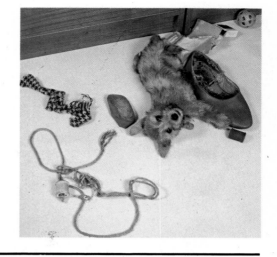

Dogs, like people, learn all the time. Every experience teaches them something, either good or bad. A puppy is learning from its surroundings most of the time and this is where you can do a great deal to influence the future behaviour of your dog. Training is not only the formal lessons which you give your dog when it is adult. It is the way you have treated the problems and pleasures of dog-owning right from the beginning.

When you first get your puppy home, remember that it is still a baby, one that has already faced the ordeal of a journey and is probably feeling rather queasy as a consequence. Do not overwhelm it with fuss and attention but let the animal explore its new surroundings in its own time. The puppy which appeared so full of bounce when with its litter mates may well be very abashed at finding itself totally alone in a place which smells unfamiliar.

First principles

If you have been wise you will first have put the puppy down either in your own garden or on sheets of newspaper so that when it produces the expected large puddle you can praise it for being in the right place. How quickly you housetrain your puppy depends almost entirely on how watchful you are. Baby animals have little control over their bodily functions and cannot wait, so you must be ready to drop everything you are doing in order to take the pup outside as soon as you see it circling and sniffing the floor. You must also be ready to stay with it so that you can praise the right action, even though rushing the animal to the right area may have served to distract its mind from the impulse. As a

The Dalmatian is a dog with a sporting past which included accompanying the horses and carriages of the rich to add a final touch of style to the turnout as it paraded through the park.

rough guide young puppies need to empty their bladder every two hours or so, particularly after a meal, a sleep or an energetic play.

When you are trying to teach your dog anything from being clean in the house to keeping off the flower beds the principles are the same. The dog can only connect your reaction with what it is doing at the time. This means that you cannot correct a dog for something it has done in the past, since the dog will not connect the crime with the punishment. Equally it is no good threatening retribution for something you think the dog might be going to do in the future. The dog lives strictly in the present and it is your praise and your blame for what the dog is doing at the time that gradually teaches the animal the behaviour you want.

Puppies under six months are too young to have formal lessons but you can do a great deal to prevent your dog developing bad habits. If you do not want your dog to climb on the furniture or sleep on the beds, then it is very much easier if you do not let it start. This means that almost the first thing you will be teaching, and also one of the most important, is the meaning of the word 'No'. This should always be growled out in a forceful way, since animals respond far more to the tone of voice than words.

A bitch with a litter not only feeds and cleans her puppies, she also plays with them and disciplines them. To a certain extent she regulates their behaviour. A puppy that is playing too roughly, or worrying her when she wants to rest, will be warned to stop with a growl. If this is ignored the bitch will then nip it hard enough to cause a yell. She will then immediately become her usual friendly self. Following her methods, an owner should growl out 'No' when the puppy is doing wrong, and if this has no effect, be prepared to follow it up with a light tap sufficient to deter the puppy. As soon as the puppy stops behaving badly, the

All puppies need toys but they need not be elaborate ones. An empty cardboard box, an old slipper or a piece of thick, knotted string will give a puppy hours of pleasure.

owner should become friendly and encouraging.

Don't say 'No' unless you are prepared to go and stop the dog doing what it shouldn't – and as soon as it has stopped you must praise it. Praise should always be given in a happy and enthusiastic manner. The more pleased you make your dog feel for doing the right thing the quicker it will learn.

Young puppies alternate deep sleep with bouts of energetic exploration and play. When they are awake they delight in human company, so make the most of this period of trust by calling the puppy to you often and making a great fuss of it when it comes. When choosing a name for your dog, try to keep it fairly short. Esmerelda, for example, may be a splendid name but it is rather too long for everyday use and a fast response from your dog. Use every chance to call the dog to you for something pleasant; its meal, a game, a titbit or a cuddle. Never call the dog to you in order to scold it. If you want to find fault, then go to the dog. A puppy must always feel confident of its welcome when it answers to its name.

New situations

Puppies get enough exercise playing and exploring their home surroundings but they also need to be taken out and about so that they meet people, other dogs and new situations. The more they see when young the more confident they are likely to be when adult. Also, teaching your dog to walk on a collar and lead is easiest when it is very young. Put a lightweight collar on your puppy as soon as it is home with you and settled in. Puppies will scratch repeatedly and scrape themselves along the ground in

Above: The check chain is a useful training aid but it must be put on and used correctly for successful results. The dog must always be worked on your left when it is wearing it.

an effort to remove a collar, but eventually forget it is there.

When teaching something new, do it in a quiet but familiar spot, which can very well be in your home with all but the largest of breeds. In the case of lead training, snap a lightweight lead to the collar and coax the puppy to follow you. Once round the room with plenty of petting is enough to start with. Some puppies will fight the new restraint, bucking like rodeo horses and even yelling with a mixture of fright and temper. If this happens to you just stand still and wait for the pup to cool down. As soon as it shows signs of stopping crouch down and call it to you so that you can give plenty of praise. Then try and coax it a few more steps. Most dogs associate the lead with the pleasures of going out, so it will not take long for a puppy to enjoy it. Always keep the dog walking comfortably beside you, jerking

it back when it gets too far forward and praising it when it is in the right position. If you make this a rule right from the start you can prevent your dog ever pulling you along.

Heavy traffic, loud noises, crowds of people – sooner or later your puppy is going to come across something that it finds frightening. When this happens do not show too much sympathy. If you pet the dog in an effort to reassure it, it will take your praise as approval of its fear. Be calm and matter-of-fact and let the dog study the situation before taking it past in an unhurried manner.

You should also begin to accustom your puppy to staying alone for short periods, starting off with ten minutes at a time and working up to half an hour or so. If you do not shut it in a pen for this period, make sure there are no dangers in the room such as electrical leads plugged in.

Teaching a puppy to be groomed

All puppies, even those with short easily managed coats, should become accustomed to being groomed at an early age. Use a baby brush and small

toothed comb, being gentle and patient. It is more convenient to groom the small and medium sized breeds on a table. This should have a non-slip surface. A heavyweight rubber mat is ideal. Lift the puppy on to the table, reassure it and make sure it cannot jump off and hurt itself while you stroke it with the brush rather than do anything more strenuous. Teach the dog to stand quietly while you brush each side. Don't let it think it's a game, with the brush as a prize. If you are going to have a puppy which will be

Below: This Bloodhound is being taught to lie down on command by being placed gently in the right position. *Right above:* Playing ball games with your dog is one way of ensuring that it gets enough exercise when space or time is limited. Many dogs become extremely enthusiastic so make sure that you are always in command of the situation. Don't let the dog nag you to continue when you have had enough. *Right below:* Most dogs enjoy praise and therefore like to show off. A daily task, like fetching the newspaper, is easily taught and very effective.

a long-haired adult, then it will be better if the dog is taught to lie down flat on its side. Do this by putting the puppy in that position and holding it there until you tell it to get up. A dog used from puppyhood to being handled this way is rarely any trouble when your vet wants to examine it, or when you want to bath it.

Many puppies are travel sick during their first car journeys. This is usually caused by nervous stress so the less fuss you make about it the better. This problem is best cured by a daily short run in the car, especially if this ends in something pleasant such as a gallop or a play. If you are really perturbed by the mess, then put the puppy in a crate or a newspaper lined box for these short journeys as your tensions will only aggravate the problem.

Be very careful about taking a dog out in a car at all in hot weather. Never leave a dog in a parked car when the sun is shining. You may think you have parked in the shade and will only be gone a short while but it takes a very little time indeed for that metal box to turn into an oven as far as an animal is concerned. Dogs cool themselves down by panting, a method which is not very efficient in the restricted air space of a car. If you have a dog that becomes very distressed or even unconscious with heat stroke, cool the body temperature down as fast as you can, if possible by plunging the dog in cold water up to the neck.

Obedience training

All dogs need to be taught basic good manners if they are not to make nuisances of themselves. Most will benefit by some more formal lessons than the everyday teaching we have been discussing. This sort of training should not be started until the dog is at least six months old, unless you have a giant breed where manhandling the size may be a problem. Don't be in too much of a hurry to start. Police and army dogs are usually eighteen months or so before their training begins. Younger animals tire too easily and cannot concentrate for very long.

To train a dog effectively you will need some special equipment including a metal slip collar (or check chain) and a 6 ft (2 m) training leash. The latter will seem very awkward to handle at first but everything is taught on the lead so that the dog is always under your control, and you will find that the extra length of leash is very necessary.

The dog is always taught to walk on your left side, an important point when you are putting on the slip collar, which must be both put on correctly and used correctly. A slip collar consists of a length

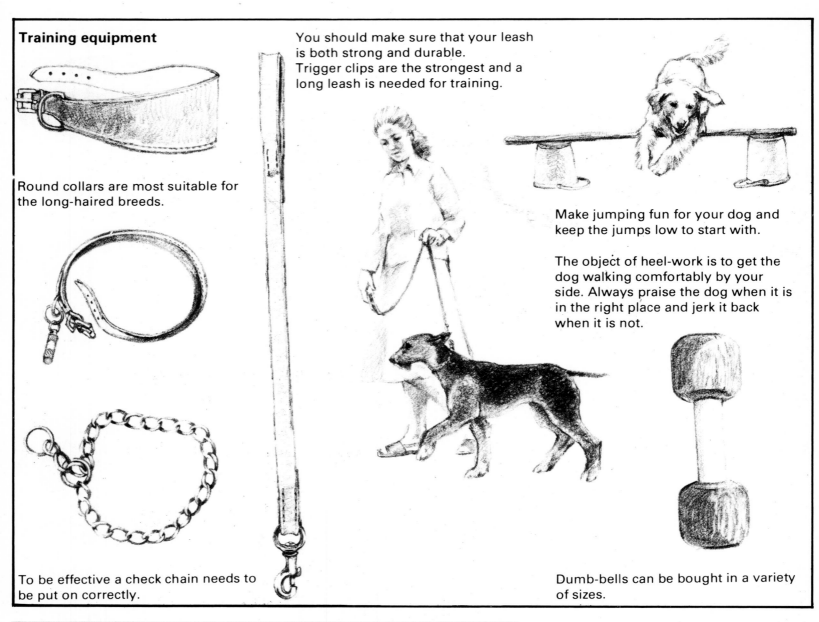

Training equipment

Round collars are most suitable for the long-haired breeds.

To be effective a check chain needs to be put on correctly.

You should make sure that your leash is both strong and durable. Trigger clips are the strongest and a long leash is needed for training.

Make jumping fun for your dog and keep the jumps low to start with.

The object of heel-work is to get the dog walking comfortably by your side. Always praise the dog when it is in the right place and jerk it back when it is not.

Dumb-bells can be bought in a variety of sizes.

of chain through one of the rings and you have a loop with one of the rings sliding along the chain. With the dog on your left, slip the loop over the dog's head in such a way that the sliding ring comes up under the dog's neck.

'Sit' and 'Heel'

Teaching your dog to sit and to walk at heel, that is quietly and steadily beside you with its head level with your body, are the first two lessons to teach. Put the training collar and leash on your dog. With the dog close to your left side, say 'Sit' and push the dog into the right position. Then walk off telling the dog to 'Heel' and encouraging it to come with you by a quick jerk and instant praise for any response. Keep the dog in the right place by praise and encouragement. The dog cannot know what you want unless you make it clear by your approval.

Left: Among the basic exercises which are taught to most working dogs, whether they are police, army or merely obedience competitors, is to retrieve a wooden dumb-bell on command.

When the animal gets in the wrong place jerk it back to your side. When the dog is beside you the lead must be slack so that the dog finds it is the only comfortable place to be. Every time you stop make the dog sit. Keep all the lessons very short but practise regularly and end each lesson with a game and romp so that both of you look forward to the session.

Once the dog will sit at your command, teach it to lie down when you say so. Again you will have to show it what you want and hold it in position until you tell it to get up. Always remember to use the same command so that the dog does not get confused. 'Alright' or 'O.K.' are good release words, telling the dog it can get up and relax. Praise it when it is in the right place. Your dog wants to please you so show it when it has.

The next step is to teach the dog to stay in either the sit or the down position while you go away, first a very short distance to the end of the leash but, later, away for longer and out of sight. Lying down and staying in the same place when you say so is probably the most important single thing you can teach your dog. To make sure that your dog is reliable, teach the whole thing very slowly and carefully, step by step, both in increasing the time and the distance that you go away. Always go back to the dog, who should be in the position in which you left him, to praise and release him.

You can also teach your dog to come when called in a more formal way and this is where your six foot leash is so useful. Leave the dog sitting, walk to the end of the leash, turn and face the dog and call it by using the dog's name and the word 'Come'. Because the dog is on the leash and under your control, you can if necessary jerk it part of the way if coaxing has no effect. Make the dog sit in front of you and be enthusiastic in your praise.

The advantages of obedience

These basic exercises can be used in many ways to ensure that your dog is a well mannered animal. A dog which can be taken anywhere without pulling on the leash is a pleasure to walk with and a dog that will come when called can have a great deal more freedom than the one who cannot be trusted. If your dog will lie flat and stay where you put it, you can make it wait before getting in or out of the car; you can leave the dog on guard while you open the front door; you can prevent the dog leaping enthusiastically on your visitors or biting the postman all by teaching him to lie down and stay when you say so.

Bad habits, like pulling on the lead, should never be allowed to develop. It is nearly always possible to teach a dog something new but not always possible to break a bad habit. Don't have a tug of war with your dog on the lead or the dog will learn to enjoy pulling. Jerk the dog back to you each time it goes too far forward and praise it enthusiastically when the lead is slack.

The Poodle (above) and the crossbred Bearded Collie (left) are both enjoying energetic games with their owners. It is a natural instinct for a dog to run after a small moving object and this instinct is encouraged when teaching a dog to retrieve a stick or a ball. Playing ball games with a very young puppy is the best way to start. Never, under any circumstances throw stones or anything liable to injure a dog's mouth. *Right:* This Cairn Terrier had a natural talent for begging and needed little teaching when a titbit was produced. Don't teach this to young puppies whose back muscles are not yet strong enough to support them in this position. Greedy dogs learn this appealing trick fastest!

Teaching your dog should be a pleasure for both of you and the more you teach it the more attentive and responsive the dog is liable to become. Dog training classes, as well as being great fun, can also be a big help. Here your dog has to learn to work with all the distractions of other dogs and people. Here you can also get expert help and advice if your dog has developed any bad habits. Training classes will also help if you decide you would like to enter the

obedience classes at shows. Each class has a series of set exercises for you and your dog to complete and most training clubs are geared to teaching you this programme. Don't forget it should be fun for both of you. Teaching your dog to jump, fetch the newspaper or a dumb-bell, or to find a hidden toy in the bushes will help build a partnership between you and your dog that is one of the best things about dog ownership.

When teaching something new praise

and enthusiasm are the rewards that your dog should work for, but the occasional titbit also helps! Once you have taught your dog basic good manners, a few light-hearted tricks can be great fun and will impress your friends. Begging on command is easy to teach but wait until the dog is adult as this places quite a strain on the dog's back muscles. Start teaching this trick by placing your dog in a corner as the angle of the walls will help its balance.

Chapter nine
The Dog Show

Dog showing is an absorbing sport for those who covet the title of champion for their dog. It entails many hours of training – a dog must pose, alert and poised, for the judges, allow itself to be handled, and move with an even and rhythmical stride beside its handler.

Dog shows are the beauty competitions of the dog world. Some show dogs are, of course, pets but most are kennel dogs, living a well organized, if rather monotonous life. To run a successful show kennel an exhibitor will certainly want to keep far more dogs than could live as house pets. Kennelling them means not only are they under closer supervision but they can also be viewed with a more critical eye than a loved and cherished house pet.

The breed standard

A dog show is where the shape, movement and conformation of one animal is compared with another. All dog breeders are striving to breed the ideal dog of their particular breed. Every breed has a written standard of excellence describing the perfect specimen and it is this breed standard which guides the judges who are making the awards.

The breed standard is approved by and lodged with the Kennel Club. Some of the standards are long and detailed but all written descriptions like these are open to a certain amount of interpretation by the person who reads them. It is this which gives dog showing its fascination. If everyone agreed which was the best dog there would be no point in dog shows at all. In practice, the handful of really great dogs on the show circuit at any one time are recognized as such by most judges and win pretty consistently. Animals of high quality who

are not quite superstars will have a more chequered career, winning one day under a judge who likes their type and being ignored another day by a judge who is impressed by something a little different. Experienced exhibitors take this in their stride, as part of the luck of the game, but some novices find this hard to understand. Very little may separate the winners, a moment's inattention by dog and handler, a dog slightly bored or a coat which has lost a little bloom, and the coveted prize card may be lost.

The first dog show was held in England in 1859. The idea rapidly caught on but

Above: Show dogs are trained from an early age to pose themselves so that they can be seen to advantage. Standing like a statue at the end of a loose lead, this Saluki attracts attention.

it was not until fifteen years later that the first American show was held. This took place in Chicago and was for sporting breeds only. 1874 also saw the first field trial which was combined with a bench show at Memphis. Since the American Kennel Club was not organized for another ten years and there were certainly no written standards, it is a little difficult to understand how these early

Left: Dog showing is a popular sport which gives many people a great deal of enjoyment. Summer shows are held in the open air with tenting in case the weather is bad. The judge examines each exhibit very carefully and small dogs, like this Yorkshire Terrier puppy, are shown on a table. *Right:* This Fox Terrier's coat will need much more trimming if it is to be shown. Currently, the Fox Terrier is not a popular breed.

Left above: A line-up of Great Pyrenees makes an impressive picture for both the judge and the ringside spectators.
Left below: All the exhibitors of long-coated breeds do most of their grooming with a brush since combing removes too much of the coat and is also liable to break the hair. Brushing is done in layers to get right down to the skin. This Bearded Collie has been trained to stay on a table while being groomed. *Right:* The show Yorkshire Terrier has a silky coat that sweeps the ground. To protect the length the hair is oiled and rolled up in paper crackers.

flocks against packs of wolves. Some of the kinds of dog that did these jobs have disappeared for good. The list of extinct breeds is quite a long one. Others have been saved by the interest of show exhibitors but a rare breed must be campaigned for in the show ring to gain the publicity necessary for its survival.

What cannot be measured in the show ring is whether the dog could still do the job for which it was originally bred. If a dog wins a prize, we can probably assume that the animal is constructed soundly enough to work. A show dog has to have a fairly equable temperament for it has to allow a complete stranger, the judge, to examine it closely and must show neither fear nor aggression. A placid, friendly temperament is an asset to a show dog and is something that most pet owners also want. However, it is not necessarily an asset in a working dog who needs drive, energy and brains. People who want working gundogs or working sheepdogs usually buy them from working stock rather than show stock. Many working dogs are not suitable as pets as they have a compulsion to work and tremendous energy, both of which need to be utilized if the dog is not to become neurotic or destructive.

Purebred dogs only

The ruling body in every country where dog shows take place is the Kennel Club of that particular part of the world. Kennel Clubs licence all shows and enforce the rules and regulations under which they are run. These differ somewhat between countries and the system described here is the American one.

Only purebred dogs can be shown and these must be registered with the Kennel Club before they can be exhibited. A purebred dog is one whose ancestry is known to consist of many registered generations of the same breed. Such an animal if mated to one of its own kind will breed true – that is it will only have

shows were judged. However, the idea certainly caught on and showing is now a very big sport with the Kennel Club licencing many thousands of shows and field trials annually.

The purpose of dog shows

Dog shows have now been in existence for over a hundred years and have steadily increased in popularity. Theoretically they are for the improvement of the purebred, or pedigree dog. Looking back over the last century one can see that the appearance of many breeds has been greatly improved and that all breeds are now much more standardized and uniform in type.

Public interest in well-bred registered dogs has never been greater and dog shows present the dog-loving general public with a chance to watch a colourful sporting event which provides the publicity that each breed requires if it is to survive. The publicity is very important, for every dog breeder depends on the sale of surplus puppies to the public as pets.

As we have seen, most breeds were working dogs of one kind or another. We no longer need dogs to drive cattle to market, pull carts or sledges, or guard

puppies that resemble the parents. A litter must be registered by the breeder who is the owner of the bitch when she was mated. After the litter registration, individual puppies may be registered either by the breeder or by the people who buy them.

Types of shows

There are various types of dog shows. An all-breed show provides classes for all the breeds which are recognized by the Kennel Club. There are also usually miscellaneous classes for those breeds which are not numerically strong enough or popular enough to merit separate recognition. In other words, the miscellaneous classes are where you find the very rare breeds. Limited breed shows, as the name suggests, confine themselves to only a certain number of breeds, while a speciality show is for one breed only.

Shows can be benched or unbenched. At a benched show each dog has a numbered place where it has to remain except when actually being shown in the ring. At an unbenched show the dogs may remain in their owner's crates or cars when not in the ring. Obviously from the spectator's point of view a benched show is much more satisfactory.

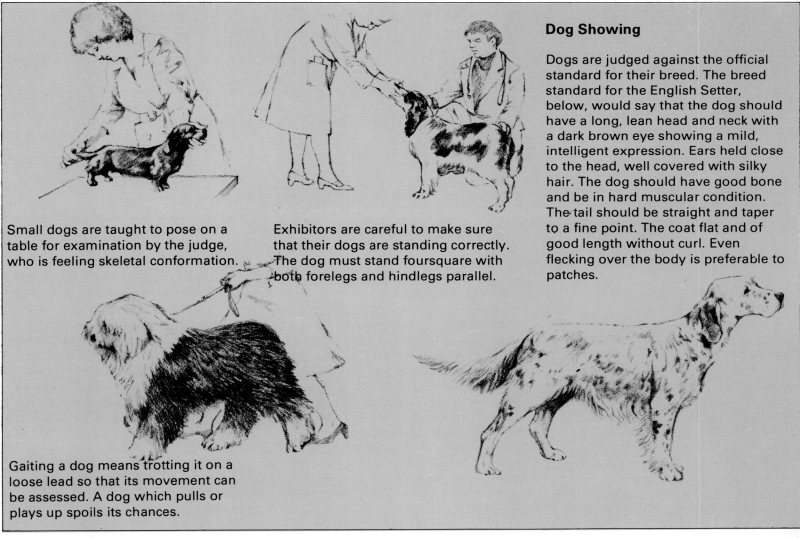

Small dogs are taught to pose on a table for examination by the judge, who is feeling skeletal conformation.

Exhibitors are careful to make sure that their dogs are standing correctly. The dog must stand foursquare with both forelegs and hindlegs parallel.

Dog Showing

Dogs are judged against the official standard for their breed. The breed standard for the English Setter, below, would say that the dog should have a long, lean head and neck with a dark brown eye showing a mild, intelligent expression. Ears held close to the head, well covered with silky hair. The dog should have good bone and be in hard muscular condition. The tail should be straight and taper to a fine point. The coat flat and of good length without curl. Even flecking over the body is preferable to patches.

Gaiting a dog means trotting it on a loose lead so that its movement can be assessed. A dog which pulls or plays up spoils its chances.

Above: The lion clip is a traditional one for the show Poodle but is not the most practical for the pet owner. The Poodle does not shed hair but the coat mats easily and needs daily brushing.

The permitted classes for each breed are Puppy, Novice, Bred by Exhibitor, American-bred, Open and the Winners Class which is made up of the first prize winners of the other classes. All these classes are divided by sex, the winner of the male classes being called Winners Dog and the winner of the classes for females being called Winners Bitch. These two animals then compete for Best of Winners who is then eligible to go into the class known as Specials Only. This is for dogs who are already breed champions. The winner of this final class is termed the Best of Breed.

A dog show is an elimination contest and the first rung on the ladder is for each breed to be judged until the Best of Breed has been decided. All the breeds recognized by the American Kennel Club are classified in one or other of six variety groups – Sporting, Hound, Working, Terrier, Toy and Non-sporting. The Best of Breeds in each group are judged against each other so that eventually there are six group winners. These final six go into the big ring to compete for the highest honour of all which is that of Best in Show. At a show like the Westminster, which is the best known of all American shows, the publicity of a Best in Show win is worth a very great deal in hard cash for the kennel involved, chiefly in advertizing.

The point system

For the dog breeder showing is an absorbing hobby where skill and effort is measured against the stock produced by others. Everyone is striving to gain the coveted title of champion for their dog. This is awarded on a points basis. A dog has to win a total of fifteen points in bench show competition to gain the title. Points are given to the Winners Dog and the Winners Bitch, the number of points won depending on the number of animals competing. The maximum number of points that a dog can win at any one show is five, so it is impossible for a dog to gain its championship in fewer than three shows, and most dogs are shown many more times before they have accumulated the necessary points.

Because of the number of shows and the distances involved in America, many shows are set up in circuits. Three or more shows may be held on consecutive days or there may be a whole string of shows held in the same area on alternate days. Many owners or breeders cannot afford the time to travel the circuits. Their dogs will be taken round by professional handlers who earn a living this way. The dogs they are showing may spend months on the road each year as their handlers follow the shows round the country.

The best shows for a novice dog and handler are match shows at which no championship points are awarded. These are much more informal events where dogs can be entered on the day and where champions are not allowed to compete. A match show does not have the same tension or long hours as a points show and makes an ideal training ground for young dogs and inexperienced handlers.

Showing techniques

Show dogs receive a lot of training and if you want to compete on equal terms it is a good idea to put some time into training your dog so that it can be seen to the best advantage. In the ring a dog will be expected to pose, standing alert and poised while the judge views it from a distance. The judge will then run his hands over the animal in order to assess its conformation. He will also expect to look at its teeth as a correct bite is an essential in all breeds. Finally movement will be taken into account. Correct movement is not the same for all breeds but it is always demonstrated in the same way with the dog trotting beside the handler, moving smartly in a straight line on a loose lead. Teaching this requires time and patience for the animal must maintain an even rhythmical stride, neither pulling nor hanging back.

Good food and the right amount of exercise are needed to get the sparkle that good condition gives. Coat care is a major consideration with many breeds and here the more you read about your breed the better. Show techniques vary from breed to breed as well so if it is possible you should watch your breed being judged before entering your dog. Remember too that win or lose there is always another day and another judge, so take your triumphs and defeats with the same good grace in the knowledge that you have been beaten by a dog properly judged as the winner.

Right: More Basset Hounds are now kept as pets and show dogs than live in packs and hunt the hare. Exhibitors get on their knees to pose these low-to-ground dogs to their best advantage.
Below: This immaculately groomed Lhasa Apso represents hours and hours of patient work with a brush. The dogs themselves learn to enjoy the fuss and attention but, if your time is limited, choose a breed with less hair.

Index

Page numbers in italics refer to
  illustrations.

Acknowledgements

The publishers would like to thank the following individuals and organisations for their kind permission to reproduce the pictures in this book.

AFA 35; Animal Photography 2-3, 16, 20 above and below, 21, 36, 37 above and below, 38, 39 above, 50, 63, 77 above (Sally-Ann Thompson) 14, 25, 27, 31, 41, 46, 54, 57, 58, 65, 66, 69, 70, 71, 73, 77 below; Ardea (J. P. Ferrero) 73; Bavaria-Verlag 60; S. C. Bisserot 9; Camera Press 21, 24; Bruce Coleman (H. Reinhard) 26, 52, 68 (J. van Wormer) 12; Colour Library International 15, 70; Gerry Cranham 74; Anne Cumbers 11, 13 above, 18, 25, 44, 72, 74, 75, 76; Christopher Davies 39; Guide Dogs for the Blind Association 32; Sonia Halliday 40; Michael Holford 7 above and below; Jacana (Labat) 1, 30 (Josedupont) 47; Keystone 39 below; John Meads 23; John Moss 6, 8, 19 above, 22, 40, 66, 67; Octopus Library (Dick Polak) 55, 56 above and below, 59 above and below, 60, 61, 62, 67; Pictor 48, 62, 64; Picturepoint 19 below; Popperfoto 33; John Rigby 4-5; Spectrum 10, 17, 29, 38, 42, 49, 63; Tony Stone Endpapers, 51; Syndication International 17, 53; Elizabeth Weiland 49; Barbara Woodhouse 45; Zefa 13 below, 28, 29, 34 (Hamilton) 43 (Mackenna) 44 (Reinhard) 11 (Villiger) 32.

PDO 81-194